George-Etienne Cartier

Montreal Bourgeois

Brian Young

McGill-Queen's University Press

KINGSTON AND MONTREAL

© McGill–Queen's University Press 1981
ISBN 0-7735-0370-6 (cloth)
ISBN 0-7735-0371-4 (paper)
Legal deposit 3rd quarter 1981
Bibliothèque nationale du Québec

Design by Naoto Kondo
Printed in Canada
Paperback edition reprinted 1985

This book has been published with the help of a grant
from the Social Science Federation of Canada, using
funds provided by the Social Sciences and Humanities
Research Council of Canada

Canadian Cataloguing in Publication Data

Young, Brian J., 1940-
George-Etienne Cartier
Bibliography: p.
Includes index.
ISBN 0-7735-0370-6 (bound). ISBN 0-7735-0371-4 (pbk.)
1. Cartier, Georges-Etienne, Sir, 1814-1873.
2. Politicians – Canada – Biography. 3. Canada –
Politics and government – 1841-1867.   I. Title.
EC471.C37Y68   971.04'092'4   C81-094874-5
F1033.C37Y68

Cover illustration: George-Etienne Cartier, 1863 (Notman Photographic Archives)

To my parents

Contents

Tables

Illustrations

FIGURES

Preface

Since his death in 1873 Cartier has had a good press. John A. Macdonald saluted him as "my second self"; an early biographer called him a "patriot, legislator, reformer, administrator, statesman, and nation-builder." Cartier remains one of "the great founders" of Canada, "the representative French Canadian." To W. L. Morton, Cartier was "the boldest, the most thrusting figure ever to appear in Canadian politics." John Irwin Cooper questioned his apparent lack of political theory and his ruthless efficiency but nationalist historians like Pierre Berton have resuscitated Cartier as the Jefferson of Confederation, "a wiry, compact and totally dedicated Canadian patriot with all the vivacity of his race." His most recent biographer describes him as a "new Napoleon," who represented "a truly national, deep-rooted and vital way of life." [1] Cartier wears a Roman toga in his bust in the Quebec legislative building; in Ottawa his statue faces Parliament; Montreal honours his memory with parks, schools, and an eighty-seven-foot statue inscribed "Above All be Canadian."

These whig interpretations emphasize the evolution of Cartier from an intemperate French-Canadian rebel in 1837 to a leader who had come to his senses, grasped Canada's destiny and by the 1840s was serving as La Fontaine's lieutenant in the achievement of responsible government and the alliance of French- and English-speaking liberals. In personality he emerges as a sort of cliché "good" French Canadian—a hard but clean player not overly aggressive but willing to compromise, a statesman imbued with *joie de vivre* and Catholic largesse, a moderate nationalist who understood that he could defend his people within a Canadian context. Unencumbered by European ideologies and respectful of British constitutional practice, he was able to adapt to Canada's unique political needs and lead French Canada into Confederation—the decisive act in Canadian history. His alliance with John A. Macdonald personified ethnic cooperation; his major business interest was the Grand Trunk Railway, itself a nation-building enterprise.

This reverence for Cartier and emphasis on his role as one of the fathers of a new liberal constitution has obstructed other interpretations. As significant as changes in the political apparatus was Cartier's participation in the transformation of Montreal civil society and in the imposition of fundamental social, economic, and legal institutions. His career coincided with the coming of steam and literacy to Quebec: he stage-managed the introduction of freehold tenure on the island of Montreal, strongly influenced railway development in the Montreal region for two decades, and was an ever-present force in a broad range of social-control measures.

The theme of the present study is that Cartier can best be understood as a Montreal bourgeois. The term is admittedly an inexact one in the context of mid-nineteenth-century Montreal where class size, sub-groups, and family linkage largely await definition. However, the term seems fitting as a functional and material framework within which to evaluate Cartier's origins, his life-style, social relations, and professional and political activities. His conservatism, his espousal of commercial expansion, British political and social values, and the ethic of thrift and hard work, his careful utilization of nationalism, and his fear of republicanism or any working-class disruption of the status quo were firmly in the tradition of a colonial entrepreneurial class. His strongest allies were the Colonial Office and its local administrators, the Grand Trunk Railway and other members of the Montreal business élite, and the Sulpicians—the very backbone of the Roman Catholic establishment in Montreal. The actions of Cartier, as an agent of the colonial, business, and religious élite, were determined by the exigencies of class conflict which, although sometimes ill-defined, formed the basis of mid-nineteenth century Montreal politics.

His career demonstrates the power of railways in nineteenth-century Montreal—if that idea needed reinforcing! For eighteen years Cartier was a minister of the crown while at the same time acting as solicitor, fixer, and friend for the Grand Trunk Railway. In the end, he was politically broken by the forces of the Canadian Pacific Railway. After his death the Macdonald government resigned, largely because of embarrassment over the presence of Cartier's hand in Hugh Allan's slush-fund till.

Cartier reinforced the La Fontaine alliance between the gallican clergy and important elements in the French- and English-speaking bourgeoisie but ultimately misjudged the competitiveness and destructiveness inherent in Canada's emerging industrial society. Montreal had changed drastically since the 1840s. Instead of being the fief of a small élite it was increasingly divided into class and ethnic ghettoes and was becoming more Catholic, more French, more industrial. Allied to traditional ruling elements—the oldest and wealthiest religious order, the senior railway, and old-line community leaders—Cartier faltered in the face of pressures generated by an aggressive ultramontane clergy, a growing urban proletariat, and a new industrial bourgeoisie replete with tough professional managers and new sources of capital. Preoccupied with national questions, a new country estate, and the illness which was to kill him, he neglected his home base and was defeated in the general elections of 1872. He died in England nine months later with the Pacific scandal breaking about him.

This work, then, attempts to put flesh on the nebulous figure of a nineteenth-century Canadian politician. Cartier's family and school experiences are reconstructed and, on the assumption that the pocketbook strongly determines actions, his evolution as a lawyer, landlord, and investor is described. His personal life offers an insight into the bourgeois society of his day: his mobility, shifting residences, and lack of traditional family life suggest a rootlessness that contrasts with the concentration of his social, professional, and investment activities within a few city-blocks in the centre of Montreal. Another potential contradiction is posed by his political role as a "national" leader and representative of a working-class constituency and his material condition as a prominent bourgeois who possessed a valet, a coat of arms, and a country estate. Cartier was at the same time a confirmed anglophile who turned increasingly to London for his clothes, his status symbols, and his ideology. In so doing, he seems to have resembled many of his peers in the French-Canadian bourgeoisie.

Given this orientation, there has been no attempt to deal with Cartier's role—admittedly important—in certain national activities that have been treated fully by his other biographers: the New Brunswick schools question, Canada's relationship with the United States, the acquisition of the west (in which he demonstrated his commitment to the development of a Montreal hinterland), and the Riel affair.[2] There are other aspects of Cartier's career concerning which the evidence is still incomplete. His association with the Canadian militia and the formation of municipal institutions are examples of areas of important social and political impact in Montreal which are treated here in marginal fashion.

To emphasize the themes of family, social position, ideology, and institutions, I have departed from a strictly chronological presentation. For this reason the chronological chart at the end of the text is important in helping the reader to integrate the various aspects of Cartier's personal, professional, and public lives.

Since Cartier's career spanned three constitutional periods, the use of certain terms, including party names and systems of exchange, has been simplified. Ontario and Quebec, while not correct designations before 1867, have been used for the period after 1840 in preference to the cumbersome Canada West and Canada East. To avoid confusion due to the frequent changes in party names during the Union era (1841–67), the term "Reform party" has been used for the period before 1854, "Conservative party" thereafter; for the same reason the term "Rouges" has been freely employed for the period 1849 to 1870. Exact terminology as well as the political machinations surrounding the name changes can be found in J. M. S. Careless, *Union of the Canadas: The Growth of Canadian Institutions* and Paul Cornell, *The Alignment of Political Groups in Canada, 1841–67*.

A leave fellowship to complete the writing of this book was granted by the Social Sciences and Humanities Research Council of Canada. Leave and a summer research grant were awarded by McGill University.

Archivists at the Public Archives of Canada and Les Archives Nationales du Québec aided generously in my research. Père Bruno Harel, archivist at the St. Sulpice archives in Montreal, was particularly helpful in opening Sulpician records as was Pamela Miller with the Cartier collection at the McCord Museum. Like so many novice cartographers, I relied on Ed Dahl, head of the Early Canadian Cartography Section at the Public Archives of Canada, for suggestions on my maps. Dr. George-Etienne Cartier gave me permission to read his collection of Cartier family papers and then installed me in his living room for several days. Two Parks Canada historians—Marthe Lacombe and Louis Richer—made the ultimate sacrifice to a fellow historian: they gave me access to their own research notes, their unpublished manuscripts, and their photocopy machine. Two friends at McGill, Bob Sweeny and Bryan Palmer, helped me shape the theoretical problems posed by nineteenth-century Canadian history. I am particularly appreciative of the collaboration of Richard Rice who read the manuscript and did his best to point out interpretative difficulties.

Chapter One
Origins

S t. Antoine, George-Etienne Cartier's birthplace, is still a tranquil
Richelieu River village. Sorel is twenty miles downstream while to
the southwest the Richelieu drains the St. Jean and Lake Champlain
regions. Montreal is thirty-six miles west. Part of the seigneury of
Contrecoeur, the St. Antoine area was cleared in the 1720s and the first
church built in 1750.[1] The village's main street stretches along the river
and the church commands a fine view of St. Denis, just across the river.
The cemetery, located between the church and the village hockey rink,
contains many Cartier graves. Parish records show that the Cartiers
first came to the village in the mid-eighteenth century; some still reside
there. Although the Cartier family home has been demolished, that of
his uncle—a few hundred yards upstream from the church—remains as
St. Antoine's most impressive home.

Cartier was born in St. Antoine on September 6, 1814, into a family
who had been merchants for three generations. The Cartiers—who had
no apparent connection with the explorer, Jacques Cartier—originated
near Angers, France. Cartier's great-grandfather, Jacques Cartier
(1720–70), emigrated to Canada in 1735 and by 1750 was an important Quebec City salt and fish merchant. He remained in Canada after
the British conquest and, despite strong competition from English
merchants, expanded into the grain trade. By the end of the century the
Cartiers had two warehouses on the Quebec City waterfront and a
wharf. Jacques Cartier's impressive two-storey house at 50 rue Saint-
Jean included a large porch, a stable, and an outdoor bake-oven. In
addition to this property Cartier owned two lots along the St. Charles
River, as well as 100 acres of rural property at Deschambault.[2]

Around 1770 Cartier's two sons moved to the Richelieu Valley where they soon prospered exporting wheat, peas, and flax. Jacques Cartier II (1750–1814) settled in St. Antoine, his brother Joseph (b. 1752) across the river in St. Denis. In 1801 Jacques Cartier II inaugurated a mail service from Sorel to St. Hyacinthe. Five years later the Cartiers disbanded the family business in Quebec City and henceforth dealt with the export house of George Symes in Quebec City and his partner Austin Cuvillier of Montreal. By the 1820s the Cartiers owned coasting vessels for the St. Lawrence trade and smaller *bateaux du roi* for use in the shallow Richelieu River.[3]

By 1800 the Cartiers' marriages, homes, political posts, military commissions, and life-style attested to their standing as important Richelieu Valley merchants. Joseph Cartier cemented the trading relationship with the Cuvilliers by marrying Marie-Aimée Cuvillier; Jacques Cartier II married Cecile Gervaise (1753–83), the product of an old Montreal family and cousin of Bishop Plessis. In 1782 Jacques Cartier II built the "House of Seven Chimneys," a seventeen-room stone building that included a store, warehouse, vault, office, three separate apartments, and servant quarters. A few years later he built an identical house for his nephew. As well, Jacques Cartier II became an important landowner by purchasing half of the concession of St. Antoine to which he added a woodlot and other properties. In 1802 he bought fifty-nine ounces of silver to decorate the family's spoon service. When he died in 1814 his estate was valued at 166,370 French livres. His moveable goods, not including the contents of his house, were auctioned for 46,122 French livres.[4]

Jacques Cartier II initiated the family tradition of political and military service. He represented Surrey (Verchères) in the Legislative Assembly, 1805–9, fought for the British in the American Revolution, and at his death commanded the Verchères militia. At least twelve Cartiers had militia appointments between 1789 and 1814: they included five lieutenants, two captains, two majors, and two paymasters.[5]

The marriage of Cartier's parents—Jacques Cartier III (1774–1841) and Marguerite Paradis (1779–1848)—united two merchant families. Although they did not have the extraregional influence of the Cartiers, the Paradis were well known in St. Antoine. Cartier's maternal grandfather, Joseph Paradis (1732–1802), was apprenticed at sea for three years but by 1750 had settled in St. Antoine as a merchant. Within a few years he had a licence to sell liquor, had bills of exchange that totalled £83,000, and was able to send his son to school in Sorel, and to marry his daughter to a Cartier. Marguerite Paradis was born in St. Antoine,

FIGURE I. Region of Montreal with place-names cited in text

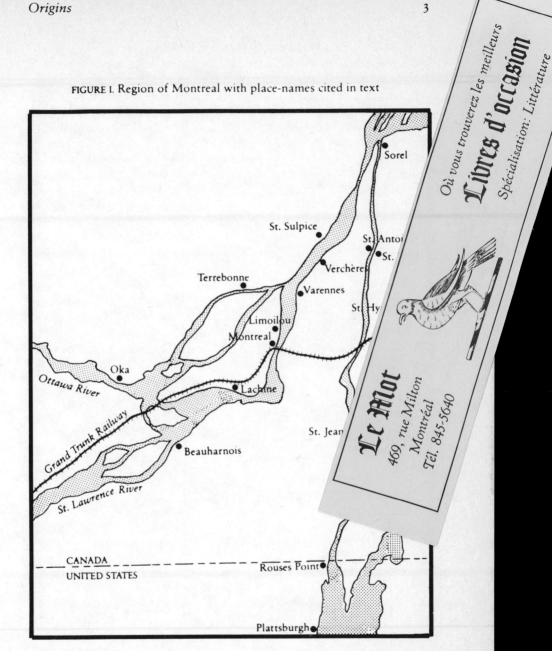

Figure 2. The Cartier Family Tree

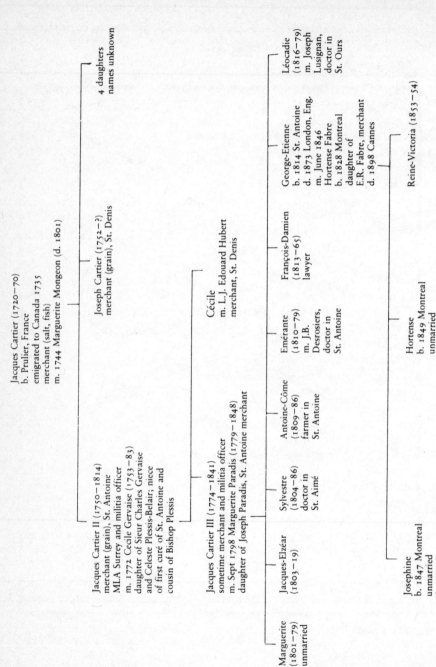

Jacques Cartier (1720–70)
b. Prulier, France
emigrated to Canada 1735
merchant (salt, fish)
m. 1744 Marguerite Mongeon (d. 1801)

Joseph Cartier (1752–?)
merchant (grain), St. Denis

4 daughters
names unknown

Jacques Cartier II (1750–1814)
merchant (grain), St. Antoine
MLA Surrey and militia officer
m. 1772 Cécile Gervaise (1753–83)
daughter of Sieur Charles Gervaise
and Celeste Plessis-Belair, niece
of first curé of St. Antoine and
cousin of Bishop Plessis

Cécile
m. L.J. Edouard Hubert
merchant, St. Denis

Jacques Cartier III (1774–1841)
sometime merchant and militia officer
m. Sept 1798 Marguerite Paradis (1779–1848)
daughter of Joseph Paradis, St. Antoine merchant

Marguerite
(1801–79)
unmarried

Jacques-Elzéar
(1803–19)

Sylvestre
(1804–86)
doctor in
St. Aimé

Antoine-Côme
(1809–86)
farmer in
St. Antoine

Emérante
(1810–79)
m. J.B.
Desrosiers,
doctor in
St. Antoine

François-Damien
(1813–65)
lawyer

George-Etienne
b. 1814 St. Antoine
d. 1873 London, Eng.
m. June 1846
Hortense Fabre
b. 1828 Montreal
daughter of
E.R. Fabre, merchant
d. 1898 Cannes

Léocadie
(1816–79)
m. Joseph
Lusignan,
doctor in
St. Ours

Josephine
b. 1847 Montreal
unmarried
d. 1886 Cannes

Hortense
b. 1849 Montreal
unmarried
d. 1941 Cannes

Reine-Victoria (1853–54)

married Jacques Cartier in 1798 in the parish church, and a year later gave birth to the first of her eight children.[6]

Cartier's parents showed evidence of the same contrast in personalities that Cartier was to experience in his own marriage. His father was gay, social, and extroverted; his mother was family and church-oriented. Although he described himself as a merchant and advertised wheat for sale in the decade after his father's death, Jacques Cartier III had little interest in commerce. Faced with his only son's distaste for the life of a merchant, Jacques Cartier II brought his nephew Joseph Cartier (1780–1844) from St. Denis, built him a large home in St. Antoine, and entrusted much of the family business to him.[7] Jacques Cartier III, with tastes that ran to clothes, music, fine liquor, and "la société joyeuse et dissipée," abandoned the routine of the warehouse for pleasures of the parlour and parade ground. He preferred seigneurs or British officers as house guests to the Récollet priests invited by his wife and was particularly proud of his rank as lieutenant-colonel and his military service with the Verchères militia in the War of 1812.[8]

Jacques Cartier's profligate life coincided with a severe agricultural crisis in Quebec that lasted for decades. As merchants the Cartiers' wealth was based on the export of wheat and on Richelieu Valley prosperity. However, wheat production in the county of Verchères declined from 2,003,664 litres in 1831 to 157,248 in 1844. The population of St. Antoine, which had quadrupled from 300 in 1750 to 1,285 in 1790, declined from 2,316 in 1840 to 1,663 in 1871.[9] Jacques Cartier III received £83,180 in capital from his father's estate, £46,122 from the sale of moveable goods plus the family home and its contents.[10] Within fifteen years the inheritance was gone and Jacques Cartier was bankrupt. In 1830 he was before the courts in a suit initiated by his wife, who apparently wanted to protect the family fortune. Describing her husband as being "insolvable" and in a state of "déconfiture," Madame Cartier was granted £1,823; unable to collect she sued again in 1840.[11]

Despite bankruptcy the Cartiers lived well. They rented three pews in the parish church, subscribed to the Montreal newspaper, *La Minerve*, and had four house servants.[12] The Cartier boys went to Montreal's most prestigious private school and all except the eldest, Jacques-Elzéar (1803–19), entered a profession: two became lawyers, one a doctor, and another a notary (see fig. 2). Sylvestre (1804–86) became a doctor at St. Aimé de Yamaska. Antoine-Côme (1809–86) was trained as a notary but became farmer-manager of the Cartier estate in St. Antoine. François-Damien (1813–65) and George-Etienne both became Montreal lawyers. Of the three daughters, Marguerite (1801–79) never married and became a well-known equestrian and prominent member of St. Antoine society; the two younger girls married doctors.[13]

Cartier was baptized George-Etienne, apparently after George III of Great Britain, but the French "Georges" was often used. Following common practice his second name was taken from his godfather, Etienne Gauvreau. Although biographers mention Cartier's attendance at a local school it seems likely that he received his grade-school education at home.[14]

In 1824 the ten-year-old Cartier was sent with his brother Damien to the Sulpicians' Collège de Montréal, an important training-ground for the Montreal-area élite and the preferred school for male Cartiers. His eldest brother had died while in attendance and another brother, Antoine-Côme, had already been at the school for two years.[15] The college had an English-speaking section and twenty-three of Cartier's classmates had English names. His graduating class produced eight merchants, five lawyers, five doctors, five notaries, and three priests.[16]

Run by priests who modelled their school on the extensive seminary system of the French mother-house, the Collège de Montréal emphasized a classical program in syntax, methods, literature, rhetoric, and philosophy. Located on St. Paul Street at the western extremity of Montreal the school had pleasant grounds, a playing field, and a brook. Cartier lived with 120 resident students in five large dormitories that, according to the college's brochure, had indoor toilet facilities.[17] School fees were $80 a year and each student provided his own mattress, bedclothes, clothesbrush, silverware, two pairs of new shoes, and two blue caps. The Sulpician régime was strict. Students wore a blue uniform with white trim and a *ceinture flèchée*. Bright vests, silver buckles, beaver boots, and white hats were forbidden. Pupils rose at 5:30 a.m. and after mass and breakfast were in class by 8 o'clock. To preserve purity, care was taken to ensure that only one student at a time was in the bathroom and special permission was needed to enter the kitchen or servants' quarters. All letters were censored and college rules obliged students to report classmates who swore, possessed distasteful literature, or had infectious diseases.[18] Students left the school only rarely; if permitted to go into town they had to return by 4:30 p.m. On Sunday they marched in pairs to mass in Notre Dame Church and once a week walked to the Sulpician farm on Côte des Neiges.[19]

Sulpician discipline did not prevent student uprisings. Just three months after the July rebellions in France and in the midst of the turbulent Lower Canadian elections of 1830, Cartier's classmates rebelled. Complaining of Sulpician insensitivity and an over-reliance on

CARTIER'S GRANDFATHER AND PARENTS:
top, Jacques Cartier II;
below, Marguerite Cartier, née Paradis,
and Jacques Cartier III

French as opposed to French-Canadian teachers, the rebels called for a charter of rights and the abolition of corporal punishment: "Respectez nos droits, sinon . . . à la révolte."[20] Students wore the tricolor, burned a teacher in effigy, and denounced the school director as a "Charles x," a reference to the recently deposed French monarch. Cartier's role is not clear but all except some of the very youngest students participated in the three-day rebellion. Among the activists were two of Papineau's sons and his nephew Louis A. Dessaulles, Joseph Duquette (executed in 1838), and Joseph-Amable Berthelot, Cartier's friend and future law partner.[21]

A superior student, Cartier took prizes in religion, grammar, and modern history and gave the valedictory address.[22] More important, however, than the prizes or formal classes was the group association and social consciousness which his seminary education reinforced. It was the Sulpicians, he remarked thirty-five years after his graduation, who "m'a instruit, discipliné, éclairé, indiqué la voie à suivre."[23] Many of Cartier's lifelong friends and business associates were among his classmates. Joseph-Amable Berthelot (1815–97) became his law partner: Charles Leblanc, sheriff of Montreal, was a close adviser concerning Montreal political affairs; Maurice Cuvillier, a businessman, looked after Cartier's financial affairs in the last decade of his life. Seigneurs of the island of Montreal and perennial supporters of established government, the Sulpicians were social and political conservatives but progressive in their economic views. Cartier became their lawyer, defended them in their long struggle with the Bishop of Montreal, promoted their interests in government circles, and supervised the transformation of their seigneurial lands into freehold tenure.

At the age of seventeen Cartier began a clerkship in the Montreal law office of Edouard-Etienne Rodier. His merchant family origins, his academic ability, and his taste for secular pleasures made this career a logical choice. Law was an expanding profession in a growing commercial centre. In 1825 Montreal had fifty-five lawyers and twenty student lawyers in a population of over 22,000.[24] The decision to article in Rodier's office was significant. A nationalist, anticlerical, and bon vivant, Rodier was the youngest member of the Legislative Assembly and he introduced his student to the patriotes Papineau, Thomas Storrow Brown, Louis La Fontaine, Augustin-Norbert Morin—and to their taverns and their ideology. From Rodier's Craig Street office, Cartier could easily slip away to meetings in the Nelson Hotel or the nationalist bookstore run by his future father-in-law, Edouard-Raymond Fabre.

The rebellions in Lower Canada had a distinct regional and class orientation with the main thrust coming from francophone bourgeois in Montreal and the surrounding Two Mountains and Richelieu regions. A young francophone lawyer and son of a bankrupt rural merchant, Cartier was typical of the social group who rallied to Papineau's banner. Crop failures, economic depression, and demographic pressures from the Eastern Townships threatened his family's business in St. Antoine. Francophone professionals in Montreal resented the English-speaking community's domination of government posts and international trade. English-speaking immigration into Montreal with its accompanying Irish Catholicism, its introduction of cholera, and its disruptive effect on the labour market added to francophone insecurity.[25] Cartier was apparently towards the conservative end of the *patriote* scale among what one historian called the "étudiants à l'esprit"— young Montrealers motivated more by concern for their professional future than by revolutionary principles.[26] Although it is difficult to isolate Cartier's own political and social ideals before 1838, his education, his refusal to participate in the second and more radical wave of rebellions in 1838, his affirmation of loyalty in September 1838, and his later political career indicate that he was not among the *patriote* element which was strongly anticlerical, antiseigneurial, and antimonarchical.

Cartier quickly became prominent as a reliable secretary and jack-of-all-trades for diverse nationalist organizations. In 1834 the twenty-year-old law student signed the manifesto of a secret society, "Aide-toi, le Ciel t'aidera," and a few months later composed and sang "O Canada, mon pays, mes amours" for the first St. Jean Baptiste celebrations:

> Comme le veut un vieil adage,
> Rien n'est plus beau que son pays,
> Et de le chanter c'est l'usage.
> Le mien, je chante à mes amis (bis).
> L'étranger voit avec un oeil d'envie
> Du Saint Laurent le majestueux cours.
> A son aspect le Canadien s'écrie (bis).
> O Canada, mon pays, mes amours.
> Mon pays, mon pays, mes amours (bis).[27]

He campaigned for Papineau and Robert Nelson in the elections of 1834 and subscribed to a relief fund for Ludger Duvernay, the jailed editor of *La Minerve*. By 1836 the St. Jean Baptiste celebrations reflected a growing *patriote* intransigence: toasts were drunk to Papineau, the United States, and Upper Canadian reformers and Cartier sang a new composition, "Avant tout, je suis canadien." In the face of tory aggressiveness and the hard-line policy of Lord Russell's Ten Resolutions, paramilitary organizations and constitutional associations were formed. Cartier participated in the *patriote* organization in the Montreal suburb of St. Laurent and was particularly active as secretary of the Central Committee for the district of Montreal.[28] This important committee expanded throughout the Montreal region, sent a petition of support to British chartists, and called for more efficient justice, improved communications, religious freedom, and the financing of schools from crown-land revenues.

The situation deteriorated rapidly in the fall of 1837. In September Cartier was among the 500 *patriotes* who met in the Hotel Nelson to form the Sons of Liberty. Modelled on the American revolutionary group, their main goal was independence. Violence was increasingly prevalent, first in Montreal and then in the countryside. In one incident the Sons of Liberty clashed with a tory "axe-handle brigade" outside Bonacina's Tavern. One *patriote* lost an eye, the riot act was read, and troops called in. Warrants were issued for the arrest of troublemakers, and Cartier, threatened with arrest, left for St. Antoine.

His return to the Richelieu Valley placed him in the very centre of revolutionary activity. On October 23 he participated in a six-county *patriote* rally in St. Charles which denounced executive oligarchy and called for the popular election of magistrates and militia officers. One of Cartier's brothers helped to organize demonstrations in Verchères County, his cousin Henri Cartier participated in the rebellions, and a Eusèbe Cartier was imprisoned in St. Hyacinthe.[29] Cartier himself spoke after mass in St. Antoine but was apparently unable to incite the villagers to rebellion since, according to one hostile newspaper, "at the muster, his regiment, including himself, numbered only four individuals."[30]

Cartier participated in the *patriote* victory at St. Denis and during the battle crossed the river to St. Antoine and returned with ammunition. After the retreat of the government forces he and Wolfred Nelson spent nine days trying to organize local resistance, felling trees across main roads, and preparing a rudimentary garrison. Local support, however, dwindled quickly. Bishop Lartique told the curé of St. Denis to refuse the sacraments to rebel supporters, *patriote* leaders like Rodier and Papineau had fled to the United States, and other leaders had been jailed. With the approach of British troops, Cartier, Nelson, and the other activists fled to a swamp near St. Denis and then separated to make their own way to exile.[31]

Despite published reports that he had frozen to death, Cartier spent the winter hidden with his cousin in a spacious farmhouse near St. Antoine. Their sojourn ended when they became over-attentive to their host's maid. Noticing two pairs of legs sticking through a stovepipe hole in the ceiling, the maid's suitor—"as jealous as a Turk"—threatened to inform the authorities.[32] Forced to flee in May 1838, the Cartiers, hidden in barrels, crossed into the United States at Rouses Point. Cartier stayed first in Plattsburgh, journeyed south to see Papineau in Saratoga, and finally joined Ludger Duvernay in Burlington, Vermont.

Performance in 1837 became an important benchmark for a generation of francophone politicians. Cartier emerged from the rebellions with impressive credentials—a decade of journeyman labours for the *patriote* cause, a charge of treason on his head, and the warm testimony of heroes like Wolfred Nelson. Like his Richelieu Valley merchant background, his Sulpician education, and his training in law, Cartier's rebellion experience gave him a strong common base with his francophone peers.

Chapter Two

Business, Family, and Social Position

Admitted to the bar in November 1835, Cartier opened a law office with his brother in Montreal's legal district. Three years later Cartier was in exile with a charge of treason on his head. Within a decade his personal circumstances had again changed dramatically. By 1848 he was an establishment lawyer, successful urban landlord, captain in the Montreal militia, married, and a member of the Legislative Assembly. Political prominence in the 1850s and 1860s as Montreal's leading Conservative brought a new scale of international clients—the church, the French government, railway, shipping, and mining companies. By the end of his career he represented the two most important religious and business corporations in Montreal and had a substantial income from urban rents, legal fees, stock dividends, and the patronage of his friends. His wealth and political position enabled him to pursue social ambitions involving a country estate, a title, a coat of arms, and frequent visits to Europe.

Cartier's early practice was general and heavily seeded with work offered by family members, home-town acquaintances with business in Montreal, a friendly seigneur, a local priest, his future father-in-law, and various small businessmen. Fracases and bankruptcies in his own family helped him establish his practice. He was paid to handle his mother's financial affairs, a cousin's law suit, his uncle's bankruptcy, and his father's succession. His first two recorded uses of the bailiff were on behalf of his father.[1] Other Cartiers hired him to prepare their wills, mortgages, leases, and contracts. To build up his practice Cartier drew on school, political, and family contacts. Early clients included Joseph Masson, the seigneur of Terrebonne, L. A. Dessaulles, a Collège de Montréal friend, and *patriotes* like Dr. Wolfred Nelson, a family acquaintance from the Richelieu Valley, E. R. Fabre, his future father-in-law, and Ludger Duvernay. He obtained a hotel licence for one client, acted as legal guardian for another, and sent the sheriff on behalf of a third.[2] In contrast to the urban orientation of his later career, a considerable portion of his early business originated in the rural parishes where his family had lived for almost a century: the curé of Contrecoeur, the neighbouring village of St. Antoine, hired him four times in 1841; Cartier acted for two local groups, the *fabrique* of Contrecoeur and the municipality of Varennes; his chief rural client, the seigneur of Varennes, paid Cartier £177 between 1841 and 1848 for regulating a boundary dispute, drawing up terms of a £2,000 loan, and bringing law suits against those who damaged his roads.[3]

By the mid-1840s the older merchant and banking élite—usually tory and English-speaking—was being challenged by younger Montrealers eager to profit from urbanism, steam, and the changed political circumstances. Manufacturers, printers, shippers, and wholesalers flourished in the narrow streets around Cartier's office along with their camp-followers—lawyers, insurance agents, notaries, brokers, and real-estate speculators. Disliked by some members of the older commercial establishment as one of those "small lawyers anxious to achieve notoriety," the self-confident Cartier, secure in the possession of impressive family and *patriote* credentials, thrived in this changing milieu.[4] A gallic version of the hail-fellow-well-met, his combination of the old school-tie with an open personality, flexible scruples, and a pragmatic conservatism suited the city's style. He organized well, knew how to delegate responsibility, and kept a tight schedule in his fifteen-hour workdays. His half-dozen law clerks were "comers" from well-placed families; his favourite notaries (Joseph Belle and Théodore Doucet) were among Montreal's busiest. While his partners handled the legwork and correspondence, Cartier was the front man, attracting business, entertaining clients, and arranging cases. His turf was the street, the backroom, the court corridor. Cartier always had a leaning toward the political component of law and early in his career developed an instinct for political influence. It was presumably not by accident that clients chose Cartier to make enquiries at the crown lands office, to prepare acts of incorporation, or to refer cases "upstairs" to La Fontaine. Indeed, when the latter went to the bench his partner and brother-in-law, J. A. Berthelot, became Cartier's associate (1853). When Berthelot in turn was raised to the bench, François Pominville became Cartier's partner (1859) and three years later Louis Betournay joined the firm. Pominville had been

FIGURE 3. Cartier's bailiwick:
central Montreal
at mid-century

Institutions

1. Notre Dame Church
2. Seminary of Montreal
3. Collège de Montréal
4. St. Jacques Cathedral
5. St. Patrick's Church
6. Bank of Montreal
7. Barracks
8. Bonsecours Market
9. Court House
10. Customs House
11. Government House
12. Parliament
13. Christian Brothers school
14. Sisters of Providence almshouse
15. Rasco's Hotel
16. Hotel Nelson
17. Donnegana's Hotel

Personal

18. Fabre bookstore
19. Fabre family home
20. Cartier family home (1848-55)
21. Cartier law office
22. Luce Cuvillier home

Properties (some purchased after 1850)

23. 42-43 St. Paul St., 30 Notre Dame St.
24. 74 Notre Dame St.
25. 82 and 84 Notre Dame St.
26. 86 and 88 Notre Dame St.

secretary of the Montreal Bar Association, was the first vice-president of the Institut Canadien-Français when it broke away from the Rouge-dominated Institut Canadien in 1858, and was a former partner of the well-known Conservative, L. O. Loranger.[5]

Cartier's account books show a rapid growth in his business between 1844 and 1846 and an evolution from wills, marriage contracts, and family business to a solid commercial practice rooted in leases, land sales, contracts, and civil suits. He seems to have handled a disproportionate number of bankruptcy actions, but perhaps this was symptomatic of the times. By the mid-1840s his clientele had stabilized among Montreal's retailers, land speculators, hotel-keepers, manufacturers, entrepreneurs, and particularly among small or medium-sized merchants like E. R. Fabre, Demoyer and Généreux, Pierre Cadieux, Beaudry and Brothers, and Louis Haldimand. Ephrem and Victor Hudon—friends, political advisers, and Cartier's best clients—were listed on his books as merchants but later became prominent textile manufacturers.

In the commercial milieu frequented by Cartier ethnic ties were apparently less important than usefulness. Montreal's small but important Italian community gave Carter substantial business. His clients included Serafino Giraldi, John Donegani, the city's most flamboyant land speculator in the 1840s, and Francisco Rasco, proprietor of the fashionable hotel where Cartier himself lived.[6] His English-speaking clientele grew steadily and included Benjamin Starnes, wholesaler and later mayor and political "bagman" for Cartier, George Hagar, an important hardware merchant, Bailey Brothers, and George Chapman. A fellow lawyer's instructions to Cartier were succinct: "All I want from you is to address the jury on the opening of the Defendant's Defence. One half the jury is French, one half English. You will not be strained as in the last case. . . . Austin [Cuvillier] will hand you ten dollars. You are marked to $20 in the last case which I shall send you some other time."[7] In 1848 he argued an important case against the Bank of Montreal for the manufacturing firm of Knopp and Noad. Three years later he began making English entries in his account book. Political prominence brought a new scale of clients. His firm drew up bond-issue forms for the European Assurance Company, initiated large debt-recovery suits for forwarding companies like the Cuvilliers, represented municipalities such as Longueuil, and acted in Rome for the Seminary of Montreal.

His law practice reflected the Montreal business community's perennial concern for transportation. His professional interest in railways dated from 1846 when he handled a suit against the Montreal and Lachine Railway. He acted in an important case involving a collision in the Lachine Canal, represented the Richelieu Company in the purchase of a steamboat, and in 1853 assumed national stature as a transportation lawyer by being named Quebec solicitor for the Grand Trunk Railway.[8]

Cartier's account books exist only for the first eighteen years of his practice (1835 – 53). As entered on his books his gross income for this period was just under £5,000.[9] However, his first years of practice were disrupted by the rebellions and then he spent a year in exile. Nor do his books make clear what he paid in office, bailiff, or travel expenses, in salaries to his brother and subsequent partners, or in shared fees with other lawyers. Certain transactions, such as Cartier family business, are not entered in his books although other documents indicate that this work—an important part of his early income—was reimbursed. Nor is it evident that the bankrupt clients carried on his books, some of whom owed large sums, ever paid.

Cartier was usually paid in cash but sometimes by cheque, four-month promissory notes, or in kind. The seigneur of Varennes settled his account by delivering thirty minots of wheat to Cartier's mother. Another client left his watch as pawn. Cartier returned it when the client, a carter, drove him to Verchères for New Year's Day. A hotel-keeper applied Cartier's fees to his lodging bill. The spittoons, oyster knives, rat traps, and razor straps that Cartier bought at Hagar's General Store were deducted from law fees owed by the proprieter.[10] In the 1850s his legal income from institutional clients escalated far beyond pawned watches or razor straps. The Grand Trunk paid him $10,000 for the period 1853 – 57, the Seminary of Montreal $1,000 in the year 1871.[11]

Cartier's relaxed political morality coupled with his increasing ministerial responsibilities and his firm's role as legal agent for large institutions led to charges of corruption and conflict of interest. A blatant case occurred in 1866 when as attorney general he was reprimanded by the colonial secretary for permitting his law partner to act for France in an extradition order was signed by Solicitor General Langevin and before French forger, had escaped custody in the United States and was arrested in Canada.[12] Held in the Montreal jail, Lamirande was defended by Joseph Doutre, a well-known Rouge. The French government hired Cartier's law partner, François Pominville. Doutre built his case around the definition of forgery under British law and charged that his client was being denied *habeas corpus*. While the case was being heard, an extradition order was signed by Solicitor General Langevin and before Doutre could take action Lamirande was removed from Canada. Despite Cartier's denial of impropriety in the extradition order, the colonial secretary was not satisfied: "... the fact that the partner of the Attorney General conducted these proceedings on the part of the French government has naturally given rise to suspicion and the conduct of the Solicitor General in obtaining the warrant whilst the case was actually under the hearing of the Judge has not as yet been by any means satisfactorily explained."[13]

Another instance of questionable ethics involved the Montreal Mining Company. By 1855 this company was plagued with stock manipulations, haphazard bookkeeping, unwarranted dividends, and a debt of £19,340 to the Commercial Bank. Cartier, a company director, acted as intermediary in one stock deal in which, as the Montreal *Gazette* put it, "the circumstances look suspicious."[14] Two hundred shares of stock were given to John Ross, attorney general of Canada and president of the Grand Trunk Railway, to encourage him to place a county courthouse at the company's mine-site in the Bruce peninsula. Soon afterwards Cartier found a mysterious buyer—purportedly Hugh Allan—who was willing to pay £1,000 for Ross's shares.[15] Angered by these manipulations and the lack of profits, company officials blew the whistle. Hugh Allan denied having bought Ross's stock and resigned as the company president. An investigative committee found, in addition to the dubious nature of the purchases, what it described as "extreme irregularity": transactions had not been entered in the company's books and dividends had been paid despite the absence of profits. Ross declared his innocence but resigned from the cabinet. Cartier said little and emerged unscathed. Sixteen years later he was still on the Montreal Mining Company board, was receiving substantial dividends, and was continuing to perform special functions. The company president enclosed a note with a director's cheque for $200: "Thompson Island which the Co. wish to acquire is not included in sale to new company and would form an asset for the shareholders of the Montreal Mining Corporation."[16]

In addition to his law practice, Cartier had a substantial income from urban rents since, like many Canadian and European bourgeois of the period, he invested his surplus capital in real estate.[17] Over a period of twenty-two years (1842–64), Cartier bought lots and houses, constructed five buildings, and renovated properties. At the age of twenty-eight he made his first real-estate investment; before his fortieth birthday he was receiving eleven assessment notices from the City of

TABLE I

Urban revenue properties 1873

INCOME PROPERTY	TENANT	ANNUAL RENT	TAXES	
			tenant pays	owner pays
30 Notre Dame	D. Monette	$300	1 month rent	—
32 Notre Dame	Dr. Arthur Ricard (residence and vaccination office)	300	1 month rent	—
42 and 43 St. Paul	J. E. Lareau (merchant)	700	—	1 month rent
74 Notre Dame	J. O. Guilmette (tailor & dry-goods store)	700	3 months' rent	—
82 Notre Dame	Bruno Labelle	400	1 month rent	—
84 Notre Dame	L. Silverman (jeweller)	360	1 month rent	—
86 and 88 Notre Dame	Mathieu and Trudel (grocers)	400	3 months' rent	—

GROSS INCOME	$3,160	$3,160

EXPENSES		
Taxes (42 and 43 St. Paul St.)	58	
Insurance (all urban properties)	136	
Repairs (approximate) (1874–75: $530; 1875–76: $509)	500	
Mortgages	0	
Depreciation	?	

TOTAL EXPENSES	694	694
NET INCOME FROM URBAN PROPERTIES		$2,466.

Source: DCP, Etat démontrant les recettes et les dépenses de la succession . . . Cartier, July 1885.

Montreal; in 1853 his handyman repaired thirty-two pairs of venetian blinds. A mixture of residential and commercial, all his urban properties were concentrated in the area where he lived and worked, either on St. Paul Street, the main commercial thoroughfare, or on Notre Dame, the major east-west artery. His preference for investments in the 1840s within this small area is clear from figure 3. The use of his buildings by doctors, lawyers, tailors, jewellers, grocers, and hotel-keepers emphasizes the concentration of the professional and commercial group in the old part of the city.[18] His acquisitions were cumulative. He never sold a property and seems to have bought with an eye to security and revenue rather than speculation. In 1873 his seven urban properties included a small hotel, a vaccination office and doctor's residence, four stores, and the workshops and apartments of several tradesmen. Revenues from these properties totalled $3,160 (1873) and after expenses his net income from urban rents was $2,466 (see table 1).

Cartier's interest as a urban landlord was reflected in his ideology. Much more than simply rents, property was equated to *la patrie*, the nation, and even the soil. He associated property with saving, civic responsibility, and the work ethic: without the goal of property ownership, people wouldn't work. Ownership brought social stability, "energy," "morality," "judgement," and "honesty." In short, property-owners constituted "l'élément qui doit gouverner le monde." For years he opposed the abolition of the upper house of the Canadian legislature, on the ground that it acted as a protector of property, and he objected to universal suffrage since in his opinion only the lazy or vicious failed to meet property qualifications.[19]

Carter himself had no difficulty in meeting the £500 property qualification for membership in the Legislative Assembly since he had received 1,200 acres of wooded land in the county of Wolfe from his parents and an undetermined amount from the estate of his grandfather.[20] By 1864, without counting interest charges, overhead, and the purchase of his home (although it later became a revenue property), Cartier's investment in urban revenue properties amounted to £11,699 ($46,806), (see tables 1 and 2).

In 1842 Cartier paid £600 for his first urban property, a house on the corner of Notre Dame and Bonsecours Streets. His tenants included a navigator and a carpenter. A year later he constructed his first building at a cost of £1,846.[21] In 1845 he paid his friend and client, John Donegani, £3,650 for a large building on St. Paul Street. Cartier immediately leased this building to the British government for use as a military hospital at an annual rent of £140 (1846–49). He later rented it as a hotel. In 1847 he paid £1,250 to construct two buildings, including a store and stable, on St. Paul Street. He purchased his own home on Notre Dame Street in 1848 and the attached house for £1,330 in 1862. One house was rented as a doctor's office and residence when his wife and daughters went to England in 1871.[22] He paid £900 for a lot on Notre Dame Street in March 1855 and nine years later spent £2,123 to construct on the site two three-storey buildings that included five stores.[23]

Restricting his purchases to his own bailiwick, he bought from

TABLE 2

Rural properties 1873

PROPERTY	MORTGAGE		TAXES	INSURANCE	INCOME	VALUE
	principal	interest				
1,400 acres (Ham Township Wolfe County)	—	—	$24	—	—	$1,900 (1882)
Country estate (Limoilou)	$4,800	$336(7%)	$25	$19	$192	$20,000 (May 1874)

Source: DCP, Etat démontrant les recettes et les dépenses de la succession . . . Cartier, July 1885.

widows, clients, and friends. Mortgage money for early purchases came from *patriotes* like L. A. Dessaulles and Wolfred Nelson; later he tapped the Cuvillier family. Busy with politics and law, Cartier left the management of his properties to associates. For at least fifteen years Joseph Laramée repaired Cartier's buildings and acted as general contractor for new construction; his junior law partner, François Pominville, handled leases, advertisements, and tenant problems. His friend and banker, Maurice Cuvillier, administered financial matters.

Cartier had a keen eye for costs. A number of his properties adjoined each other, allowing the lumping of stable, cesspool, and courtyard facilities. Except for one urban property and his country estate his tenants were responsible for all taxes. Cartier himself was often tardy in payments to the water company, banks, and other creditors; in 1865 the sheriff of Arthabaska wrote in some embarrassment to remind Cartier, a cabinet minister, that he was in arrears in his payments for crown land. Fond of life in fine hotels, Cartier did not hesitate to rent his own quarters during lengthy absences. His Ottawa apartment was taken temporarily by his Conservative colleague, Alexander Campbell, and his Montreal home was leased on two occasions. In one instance he retained a main-floor campaign office and a third-floor storage area. A stringent landlord, Cartier tried to persuade British authorities to install storm windows on the building they rented as a hospital.[24] He took a mortgage on property in Châteauguay from a tenant who was in arrears. Although his country estate was not primarily a revenue-property Cartier drew up a careful lease concerning grazing, fruit trees, and the equal division of farm produce between tenant and proprietor. The tenant was responsible for local public works on the road and ditches; Cartier paid the taxes and contributed to the parish church.[25]

TABLE 3

Portfolio of stocks, bonds, and bank deposits 1873

STOCKS AND BONDS

Company	No. of shares	Face value	Paid up	Dividends	Evaluated by estate
Grand Trunk Railway (7 per cent debentures, 1859)	—	$1,000	100%	0	0
City Bank	109	10,900	100	708	10,900
Banque du Peuple	146	5,600	100	244	7,847 (1874)
Victoria Skating Rink	1	50	100	0	50
Canadian Railway Equipment Co.	100	10,000	25	123	2,500
Maritime Bank	50	5,000	10	7	500
				$1,082	$21,797

BANK DEPOSITS

Bank	Deposit
Bank of Montreal	$4,155
Bank of Montreal (London)	75
Banque d'Epargne	55
	$4,285

Note: Consols and Montreal Mining Co. stock excluded: interest from these, 1871–72, was $3,164.

Source: DCP, Etat démontrant les recettes et les dépenses de la succession . . . Cartier, July 1885.

CARTIER'S MILIEU: *below*, Bonsecours Market, St. Paul Street, Montreal; *opposite*, Fenian Raid volunteers, Champ de Mars parade-ground, Montreal, 1866

His only incongruous transaction was the purchase of 200 acres of crown land in the same township as the 1,200 acres given to him by his parents in 1841. Purchased in 1864, this holding was not urban, revenue-producing, or recreational. Unsupervised and undeveloped, it was stripped of its wild cherry timber by local farmers.[26]

Although it has been argued that French Canadians preferred property investments—at least in the 1820s—a transition during the nineteenth century from real estate to commercial and industrial stock investments was typical of the bourgeoisie in France.[27] This pattern is evident in Cartier's investments. By 1865 he had stopped buying real estate (his country home excepted) and was investing his surplus capital in stocks—primarily banks with a minor interest after 1872 in a railway equipment company. This transition appears to have been gradual and not unlike what Alberto Melucci calls the "osmose entre la propriété foncière et la bourgeoisie industrielle."[28] Before 1865 he held stock in the Montreal Mining Company and the Grand Trunk Railway but since he acted as a director of the former and solicitor for the latter it is not clear that he paid for these shares or that they represent a bona-fide interest in stock investments. Nor, despite a growing interest in the stock market, did Cartier ever sell any real estate to raise capital. By the early 1870s his income from rents was approximately double his income from stock dividends. In 1873 his one industrial stock (Canadian Railway Equipment Company) represented 9 per cent of his stock-market investment (see table 3).

TABLE 4

Income 1873

SOURCE	AMOUNT
Salary, government minister	$5,000 (1871)
Law income	?
Farm products (country estate)	192
Rents (before expenses)	3,160
Dividends and interest	1,435[1]

Source: DCP, Etat démontrant les recettes et les dépenses de la succession ... Cartier, July 1885.

1. Dividend and interest income for 1871 was $2,606 and $1,495 in 1872.

Cartier had bank accounts at the Toronto, Ottawa, and Montreal branches of the Bank of Montreal and the Quebec City branch of the Bank of Upper Canada, but after 1865 the brokerage firm of Cuvillier and Company were his main financial advisers. Maurice Cuvillier chose Cartier's portfolio, paid his bills, and permitted him substantial overdrafts. In 1868 Cartier borrowed $2,800 from Cuvillier for a nine-month period and when he died five years later he had an outstanding eighteen-month loan of $2,071 on which no interest had been paid (table 5). Cuvillier's letters to Cartier encompassed both friendship and financial advice.

> The enclosed letter from Luce undoubtedly gives you all the news of the day and which leaves nothing for me to add except to write to enclose certificates of 53 shares of City Bank stock for your account (May 5, 1865). . . . I enclose bank draft for $84 being for Miss Symes bill, St. Louis Hotel and $25 lent her. . . . I also enclose certificates on 19 shares of City Bank transferred to you which I bought at 92 being 7% discount (July 29, 1865). . . . I have invested $1199 in Peoples Bank shares . . . we are well at home (Feb. 13, 1871). . . . Will I give Lachapelle 300 dollars to pay his men? (telegram, May 27, 1871)[29]

Under Maurice Cuvillier's tutelage Cartier began investing heavily in the City Bank and la Banque du Peuple. Between April and October 1865 he bought $5,275 worth of City Bank stock, much of which he financed by selling stock in the Bank of Upper Canada ($1,506) and the City and District Bank ($1,408). His portfolio five years later was still heavily concentrated in la Banque du Peuple ($5,600) and the City Bank ($10,900). In July 1872 he paid a 10 per cent instalment on Marine Bank stock with a face value of $5,000 and four months later bought 100 shares in the Canadian Railway Equipment Company. Cartier continued to receive significant dividends from his 560 shares in the Montreal Mining Company ($2,240 in 1871). He had the same number of "Consols" shares which paid a dividend of $924 in January 1872. Since the latter two stocks were clearly indicated in his portfolio with Cuvillier and Company and yet neither appeared in his estate they were presumably "patronage" stocks which were withdrawn at his death.[30]

Family matters in St. Antoine could not be neglected despite Cartier's flourishing career in Montreal. The Cartiers were proud, prickly, and bankrupt; the prosperity of their community and more particularly, the

TABLE 5   —

Estate

ASSETS

IMMOVABLE PROPERTY		VALUE	MORTGAGE	
30 Notre Dame			0	
32 Notre Dame			0	
42 and 43 St. Paul			0	
74 Notre Dame			0	
82 Notre Dame			0	
84 Notre Dame			0	
86 and 88 Notre Dame			0	
Total purchase price of urban properties, 1840–64		$53,206		
Appreciation: urban properties		?		
1,400 acres (Wolfe County)	(1882)	1,900	0	
Country estate (Limoilou)		20,000	4,800	
		75,106		$75,106

MOVEABLE PROPERTY			
Ottawa: furniture		800	
wine		200	
Montreal (home, law office, and country estate):			
furniture and effects		2,280	
library		1,843	
silver, chandeliers, and other effects removed by wife's family		1,000 (est)	
		6,123	6,123
Stocks		21,797	21,797
Bank deposits		4,285	4,285
TOTAL ASSETS			107,311

DEBTS

Marquise de Bassano (Clara Symes)[1]		
personal loan (1865)	10,000	
outstanding interest	3,600	
Maurice Cuvillier[1]		
personal loan (1871)	2,071	
outstanding interest	238	
Seminary of Montreal[1]		
three commutations	1,148	
outstanding interest	585	
Robert Turcotte		
mortgage (country estate)	4,800	
outstanding interest	0	
Banque d'Epargne		
loan	1,216	
	23,958	23,958
REAL WORTH		83,353

Source: DCP, Etat démontrant des recettes et les dépenses de la succession . . . Cartier, July 1885.

1. Neither interest nor principal payments made before Cartier's death.

family's social position, were seriously threatened by the thirty-year agricultural depression. Cartier had to contend with aging, bankrupt parents, an alcoholic brother, and a neurotic spinster sister. In 1841 his father fell ill with fever, diarrhea, and "inflamed internal organs." Although busy with La Fontaine's Terrebonne election campaign, Cartier made two hasty trips to St. Antoine and on the second occasion buried his father with as "splendid and as solemn a funeral as possible."[31] Bankrupt for a decade, Jacques Cartier left a bickering family, pending lawsuits, and unanswered letters from sheriffs and notaries. As administrator of his father's estate Cartier arranged guarantors for the debts, sold family property in Quebec City, advanced money to his brother, sued longtime debtors of his father, settled outstanding seigneurial dues, and paid interest on overdue accounts. Division of the estate was complicated. One property measured 547 acres; others had choice river frontage, a town location, or valuable buildings.[32] One brother wanted the land closest to the church, another contested an equal division of family debts. Before his father's death Cartier had become his mother's lawyer and over a period of eight years advanced her £1,188 to pay off debts, make house repairs, and buy furniture. Transactions between mother and son were conducted in strict business fashion: advances were given in return for promissory notes, interest was charged, and the total debt notarized some months before her death.[33]

Nor were the family's concerns strictly financial. Cartier's sister, Marguerite, had remained a spinster in St. Antoine. Her brother feared she would go mad and run through the streets with her inheritance.[34] Other family members leaned on Cartier for favours and patronage. One brother wanted a job in the civil service; a cousin asked him to make enquiries at the sheriff's office. His brother Sylvestre, a country doctor, wanted Cartier to find him a government post and a rich wife. "If you open doors, let your brothers in first . . . if you want me to marry before cholera gets me, find me a girl or a widow with 60,000 francs."[35]

More serious was the drinking of his brother Damien. The two had established their law practice in 1835 as "Cartier and Cartier." However, in 1840 Cartier had Damien sign a statement declaring that they had never had a formal partnership and that Damien's remuneration had been granted solely by "la liberté et générosité de son frère."[36] By 1850 Damien was practising law only sporadically and Cartier had formed partnerships with more reliable associates. Damien's landlord sent his hotel bills directly to his brother. After a respite in St. Antoine Damien returned to live in the Richelieu Hotel in Montreal and in 1855 may have handled a few cases for his brother. However, he was soon back in St. Antoine consuming "une petite fortune" and periodically being "mis à la porte dans un état d'ivresse" by members of the family.[37] When he died in 1865 he was living with his sister in St. Antoine.

Cartier was thirty-two when he married. This relatively advanced age was considered normal for an ambitious *cavalier*, as was his emphasis on wealth and standing rather than romantic attachment: "les jeunes cavaliers d'aujourd'hui ont 30 ans. On exige, avant tout, de la fortune. Les mariages d'inclination sont aussi rares qu'en Europe."[38] Refused by Mlle. Debartzch, the daughter of the Seigneur of Contrecoeur, Cartier chose his wife, Hortense Fabre (1828–98), from an important Montreal commercial family. Her father, Edouard-Raymond Fabre (1799–1854), had been hired by Hector Bossange who came to Canada in 1815 to open the Montreal branch of the world-wide chain of Bossange bookstores. After marrying Fabre's sister, Bossange returned to France, leaving Fabre in charge of the Canadian business. Developing strong ties with both the clergy and liberal intellectuals, Fabre built the bookstore into a major importing, printing, and retail operation. He became mayor of Montreal, director of a bank and a British insurance company, and invested in newspapers, railways, and telegraph companies; in 1854 his estate was valued at £15,941.[39]

His wealth enabled him to provide his children with a comfortable Montreal life, a nine-room home at the corner of St. Lawrence and Craig streets, four servants, and trips to New York and his sister's chateau in France. His sons entered the law, the clergy, diplomacy, and journalism. Hortense was educated by the Ursuline nuns in Trois-Rivières and was then tutored in French, English, and dancing. The Fabre piano, the most expensive piece of furniture in the house, was kept in a second-floor salon; Hortense's piano teacher visited the Fabre home three times a week. Her mother, Luce Perrault Fabre, was, like other women of her standing, active in Catholic charities. She visited the poor in their homes, organized bazaars, attended retreats, and was a founding director of a Montreal orphanage, l'Institut des filles de la charité.

Cartier had known the Fabres since 1834. His law office was just a few doors away from their bookstore, a focus of intellectual and *patriote* activity. Like Cartier, Fabre had fled Montreal during the rebellions. In 1839 he helped the young lawyer re-establish his practice by giving him ten legal cases; before his marriage Cartier handled a total of twenty cases for Fabre. When Cartier's father died in bankruptcy in 1841, Fabre (along with Joseph-Amable Berthelot) acted as guarantor for the heirs. Cartier and Fabre later served together on the board of the

Montreal City and District Savings Bank. Fabre lent money to his son-in-law: in 1854 the latter was one of Fabre's biggest debtors with outstanding loans totalling £227.[40] Fabre was pleased with his daughter's marriage and told his sister that although Hortense's education had been expensive "nous la marions avantageusement." "Toujours un ami de la maison," Cartier was an "excellent avocat" of whom "brillantes affaires" could be expected.[41]

The Cartier-Fabre marriage contract included a strict "separation of property" agreement. Hortense had no dowry and her clothes, jewellery, and other personal belongings were not of sufficient value to merit a formal inventory. Her only call upon her husband's estate was an annual allowance of £100 that was secured by a special mortgage on the Cartier house at the corner of Notre Dame and Bonsecours Streets.[42] This separation of property clause may have been included to protect any encroachment by Cartier upon his wife's inheritance; in 1854 Hortense appears to have inherited one-fifth of her father's estate. The contract did, however, permit Cartier in his 1866 will to exclude his wife from any share in his estate beyond the £100 a year specifically guaranteed to her.

The morning wedding ceremony was held on June 16, 1846, in Montreal's Notre Dame Church and was performed by the curé of Contrecoeur who had hidden Fabre during the rebellions.[43] After the reception the wedding party—which included Cartier's mentor La Fontaine and his friends A. N. Morin, Wolfred Nelson, Lewis Drummond, Maurice Cuvillier, and Joseph-Amable Berthelot—went to the Laprairie railway station to see the newly-weds off on a three-week honeymoon in New York and Washington.

The marriage was not a success. The Cartiers were drinkers, dancers, and flirts. Pragmatists and third-generation bourgeois, they were at home in the rough-and-tumble secular society of the St. Lawrence Valley. For their part the Fabres were intransigent nationalists and strong Catholics. Sober and ambitious, they were reputed to have a hereditary streak of malice.[44] While the generation of Cartier's father lost a merchant fortune, Edouard-Raymond Fabre, the son of a carpenter, spent a lifetime amassing prestige and wealth for his family. Politically, the marriage became an embarrassment for both families. While Cartier accepted La Fontaine's conservatism, his father-in-law remained an incurable *patriote*, annexationist, and Papineau supporter. In 1854 Cartier sided with Wolfred Nelson in the mayoralty campaign against Fabre. Hortense's brother, Edouard-Charles, became the first archbishop of Montreal and another brother, Hector, although he studied in Cartier's law office, became a vociferous political opponent, founded an opposition newspaper, *L'Evénement*, in 1867, and ran against the Conservatives as candidate for the Parti National in 1873. Until 1858 Fabre's law partner was Louis-Amable Jetté who defeated Cartier in the elections of 1872.[45]

Cartier's 1866 will, his alliance with Luce Cuvillier, and the diaries of his daughters provide ample evidence of the failure of the marriage. Pious, caustic, and fourteen years younger than her husband, Hortense had no love for crowds, her husband's politics, or the cronies he brought home. According to one critical family friend, Hortense would have been happiest in a convent—provided she could have been the Mother Superior.[46] Her daughters' diaries show that Madame Cartier had strict opinions concerning men, their morals, and their social acceptability for her daughters. At a school graduation she remarked that convent girls were well behaved because "no bachelors were admitted there."[47]

For his part Cartier was irreverent as a young man, preoccupied in his later years with politics and another woman, gregarious throughout his life. In 1841 he boasted of caning a client who, in his words, threatened to give him "des coups de pied dans le Q." Cartier duelled, got in a shoving match with a judge at the Montreal Skating Club, "screamed and whooped" during a singsong at the governor general's residence, borrowed a colleague's residence, and according to La Fontaine left it "dans un état horrible et de mal propreté." One observer noticed his brusque treatment of the servants at a noisy dinner-party: "The dinners out here last hours, and there is such quantities of food on the table. Mr. Cartier sang or croaked after dinner, and made every one he could find stand up, hold hands, and sing a chorus. The wretched servants brought in tea, and he pushed them away till after his song was over. He pushed one on his arm lightly, and I saw the servant rubbing his arm much annoyed, and looking like a dog with a trodden-on tail."[48]

Although rumoured to have been drunk in the assembly on one occasion, Cartier never drank with Macdonald's intensity or morosity. A restless and sociable individual, he liked convivial Saturday evenings, parties, champagne, laughter, and folksongs. He relaxed after work by sending out for drinks or by playing the piano, and when in Montreal ate dinner almost every evening with associates like Louis Archambault, Sheriff Charles Leblanc, or François Pominville. A compulsive worker, he travelled incessantly. After arriving on the night train he often sent his baggage to his home and went directly to his office for a day's work.[49] He seems never to have been at ease with family life, the piano lessons of his daughters, or austere Sunday dinners with his brother-in-law, the priest.

Cartier's expansive, other-directed nature is suggested by his residences (see Chronology). He was born in a large, open home that had three apartments and sixteen inhabitants and at the age of ten was sent to live with 120 boys in the dormitories of the Collège de Montréal. At twenty-two he was living in Rasco's Hotel, a colourful establishment where actors, lawyers, officers, and their ladies dined on Italian cuisine. Cartier lived at Rasco's for ten years until he and his bride moved into the Hotel Donnegana in 1846. Described as "palatial," the newly opened Donnegana's was the Cartier home for almost two years; their first daughter was born during their residence there.

In 1848 the Cartiers moved one block east along Notre Dame Street into a fine three-storey stone house for which Cartier paid £1,600. A choice location on the eastern fringe of the commercial district, it had a view of the port and St. Lawrence from the back bedrooms.[50] The four-block walk to his office took him by the houses of friends like John Donegani, the market, his St. Paul Street properties and Rasco's Hotel (figure 3). The house itself was ten years old, large and comfortable with a dumb-waiter system connecting the dining-room to the basement kitchen. The wine cellar, larder, coal-room, and servant sleeping-quarters were also in the basement. Cartier's handyman supervised the installation of gas lighting, green shutters, a renovated fireplace in the master bedroom, and a new stove in the nursery. The main floor had eleven-foot ceilings and was dominated by a large library and parlour. The second floor contained the music room and the governess's room as well as the bedrooms.

Once elected to the assembly Cartier spent the sessions in Toronto, Quebec City, and finally Ottawa. Accustomed to hotel living and an ambulatory life-style, Cartier was probably less upset than other politicians by the periodic rotation of the assembly between Toronto and Quebec City. When in Toronto he stayed at Beard's Hotel or at Mrs. Dunlop's on Bay Street and, for at least one period, his wife and daughters joined him. He lodged at Sword's Hotel in Quebec City until the 1860s when he and Sandfield Macdonald rented quarters in the upper town in a townhouse owned by Judge Jean Duval. After 1867 he leased a four-bedroom home in Ottawa at the corner of Maria and Metcalfe Streets for an annual rent of $320. He retained an office in his Notre Dame Street house but when in Montreal slept at his country home.[51]

Cartier's marriage was undoubtedly not helped by his lifelong appreciation for the female form or what he described as his favourite occupation, "activity of the heart."[52] Before his marriage he and his friends joked about their success with girls, the quality of Quebec City women, and the relationship between a girl's education and the number of her children. Exiled in 1838 Cartier told a friend that the Montreal girls he had met in the United States were "rien d'extraordinaire." In Vermont he visited "la célèbre Madame Turtore" but "elle n'est pas bien drôle quant au physique."[53] After his marriage Cartier remained quick with a compliment for the ladies and was always among the first on the dance floor. For several years he corresponded with Lord Carnarvon's niece whom he had met in England in 1858. Cartier found her "gracious," "brilliant," and "attractive." He sent her a book and Indian embroidery; she asked for his photo, painted his portrait, and invited him to visit her in London.[54]

Given the partners' differing social attitudes, interests, and personalities, the Cartier marriage became one of form rather than substance, and husband and wife led increasingly separate lives long before his alliance with Luce Cuvillier. One author dates the couple's informal separation from the birth of their third child in 1853; certainly Cartier was absent from the baptism of this daughter.[55] When his law partner asked the Cartiers to be godparents, Cartier sent his brother-in-law to assist Madame Cartier at the ceremony. By the late 1850s the Cartiers rarely appeared in public together. In the 1860s the relationship deteriorated completely, although Madame Cartier did continue to appear with her husband at important official functions such as those connected with the Quebec Conference.[56] In a family photograph taken of Cartier and his daughters, Madame Cartier is noticeably absent. Cartier rarely slept at the family home. When he did spend four nights there in January 1871 he was an unwelcome guest; his departure, according to his daughter, was "la seule bonne nouvelle." Cartier's business relations with his wife were handled by his law partner who arranged her travel plans, bought her boat and train tickets, and accompanied her to the station.[57] By 1871 Lady Cartier lived largely abroad, visiting London, Paris, and her uncle's chateau in the Loire. After her husband's death she never returned to Canada, and ultimately settled in a villa at Cannes on the French Riviera.

Embittered and alone, Lady Cartier's main preoccupation was preparing her two surviving daughters for marriage. The youngest daughter, Reine-Victoria, died at the age of thirteen months in the cholera epidemic of 1854.[58] Josephine (1847–86) and Hortense (1849–1941) had convent educations followed by lessons in dancing, piano, German,

Spanish, and riding. In contrast to their father's casual religious practices both girls, even as young adults, attended mass almost every day;
in 1873 their uncle was named a bishop. Although the family had a pet
dog and birds the atmosphere of the Cartier home was sombre.
Josephine described 1870 as a year "replète de contrariétés amères."[59]
Hortense practised the piano for two hours every day; in the evenings
the girls sewed with their mother, spent "soirées endormitoires" with
family friends or visited their maternal grandmother for "l'inévitable
repas de famille assaisonné d'épigrammes et de regards sévères de l'abbé
qui veut nous marier."[60] British officers played an important role in the
social life of the Montreal bourgeoisie and the Cartier girls often joined
the young Hingstons, Drummonds, Tuppers, and other peers at garrison
balls or toboggan parties. Summer holidays included a week at
Cacouna, a St. Lawrence River village near Rivière de Loup, where they
joined summer-colony residents like the Galts in boules, chess, cards,
riding, or walks along the beach. Travel to Europe did not impede the
proper education of the Cartier girls. Pianos were rented, language and
riding lessons arranged, and suitable bachelors invited for tea. In
1871–72, for instance, the girls went to the theatre in London, spent a
day trying on dresses in Paris, and holidayed at their great-uncle's
chateau.

Except when the family gathered in London in the last months of his
life Cartier did not spend extended periods of time with his daughters.
He often expressed regret at not having a son to inherit his title and
confided to Macdonald: "I wish one of my girls was a son."[61] The
diaries of both girls reflect that they sided with their mother concerning
their father's life-style, his liaison with Luce Cuvillier, and his conflict
with the Fabre family. Both referred derisively to their father as "le
Capitaine" or "el Capitano" and disliked his impatience and vanity:
"1000ième répétition des mêmes intéressantes histoires, notwithstand-
ing their lack of success, mail day, more fire than ever, Thomas Thomas
[the servant] sur tous les tons de la gamme, pour envoyer des lettres par
le courrier, toujours au dernier moment."[62]

Caught in the contradiction between her parents' failed marriage and
their insistence that the institution of marriage represented the only
acceptable form of status and security for a woman, Hortense reacted
by including a bitter "notice to fathers" in her diary:

> Avis aux pères de famille: ayez en deux et accusez les quotidienne-
> ment d'être deux de trop, parlez leur toujours de vous, grondez les
> sans cesse, si ce sont des filles, mettez à la porte tous les jeunes gens

qui voudront bien vous en débarrasser en les épousant, puis accusez
les de rester vieilles filles, parlez mal devant elles de toutes celles de
leurs amies qui se marient bien ou mal, soying [sic] sûr que vos filles
ne désireront jamais ni le mariage, ni le couvent, ni la potence
comme moyen de se défaire de votre aimable société. . . This is
written on a really, really very merry Christmas 25 December,
1872.[63]

Neither girl succeeded in attracting what their mother described as "le
type du parfait gentilhomme."[64] Both remained spinsters and after their
father's death moved with their mother to the French Riviera.

In the last years of his life Cartier lived with his wife's cousin, Luce
Cuvillier (1817–1900). Her father, Austin Cuvillier (1779–1849),
was a prominent merchant, a founder of the Bank of Montreal, a
supporter of Papineau until 1834, and first speaker of the Legislative
Assembly of the United Canadas. His sister married George Symes,
reputedly the wealthiest merchant in Quebec City. Symes and Cuvillier
acted as forwarding merchants for Cartier's father and grandfather in
their Richelieu Valley grain business. Like Cartier, the Cuvilliers adjusted effectively to the changing nature of capitalism in Montreal. Two
of Luce's brothers, Maurice and Austin, had important interests in
Upper Canadian trade, banking, transportation, and real-estate development. In 1850 Maurice Cuvillier owned sixteen Montreal houses
and five stores, and was part-owner of the steamboat *Ste. Hélène*.[65] He
founded a stockbroking firm and was a director of the Metropolitan
Bank and the Montreal and St. Jérôme Colonization Railroad. Cartier
was Maurice Cuvillier's classmate at the Collège de Montréal, acted as
lawyer for the Cuvilliers as early as 1857, and by the mid-1860s had
entrusted his financial affairs to Cuvillier and Company.

Although they avoided a public scandal the Cartier-Cuvillier liaison
was well known. Journalists said little besides noting Madame Cartier's
absence and "Mlle Cuvillier's" presence at social functions attended by
Cartier. Privately, colleagues like Hector Langevin gossiped about
Cartier's brazenness.[66] The delicate problem of his Montreal address
was solved by naming Ottawa as his official residence. Montreal correspondence was sent to his law office. When in England with Cartier,
Luce probably lodged officially at the Cuvillier house in London; visits
to Cartier during legislative sessions in Quebec may have been made in
the guise of chaperoning her niece. She sent news to Cartier in Ottawa
via her brother and urged Cartier to be discreet in his letters: "My
dearest . . . you must be more particular in writing your letters. Keep all

your endearments for your————, write me business letters and nothing more."[67]

The liaison dated from at least the early 1860s. Luce became guardian for her wealthy niece, Clara Symes, in 1861. Two years later Clara Symes gave Cartier $10,000, and although this was officially a loan neither interest nor principal was paid in Cartier's lifetime. By 1864 his law partner was sending him news of Luce; during the sessions of 1864 and 1865 she visited him in Quebec City; in May 1865 she forwarded him "all the news of the day." In his 1866 will Cartier named Luce Cuvillier, paid tribute to her "sagesse et prudence," and bequeathed her $600. The will attacked his wife, her family, and their values; he urged his two daughters to follow Luce's "advice" and stipulated that they would lose their inheritance if they married any member of his wife's family.[68]

By the end of the decade Cartier and Cuvillier were living together. Between 1866 and 1873 they were in Europe together three times. Luce was in London during Cartier's trip to England in 1866, accompanied him to Europe in 1868, and was in London when he died. Cartier bought her jewellery in Paris and a table muff, riding gear, and furs in London; they bought a marble bust in Naples in 1867. Luce managed the employees at the country estate and in 1871 laid off the gardener for the winter.[69] Although Cartier apparently promised his Sulpician friend, Joseph Baile, to break off the liaison, it was Luce Cuvillier rather than Lady Cartier, who was also in London, who attended Cartier's funeral service at the French chapel.[70] At the auction of Cartier's estate, the Cuvilliers bought furniture worth $481; Lady Cartier expressed her sentiments towards the material remnants of her marriage in a letter to her husband's executors. Aside from a few personal belongings, she wrote, "Je ne veux rien absolument garder de mon ménage."[71]

Eleven years older than Cartier's wife, unmarried, and an unorthodox romantic, Luce Cuvillier smoked, wore trousers, and read Byron's poetry and the novels of George Sand.[72] At the same time she tutored girls at the Sacre Coeur convent and helped direct the same orphanage as Cartier's mother-in-law. She was bitterly attacked by the Toronto *Globe* for her role in converting her rich niece to Roman Catholicism:

> The Roman Catholic priests, ever on the watch for rich heirs and heiresses, have made a grand catch in the daughter of a late wealthy citizen of Quebec. She is about to become a nun, and thereby secures to Mother Church a million of dollars. The girl is

Hortense Cartier, née Fabre, c. 1860

Luce Cuvillier, 1865

only 17. Her relatives in this city have done all they could to prevent her taking this irreversible step but no, her spiritual advisers have conquered, and she to a nunnery goes. No one supposes that her departed father ever dreamt that the wealth he for many years toiled for, was to go in such a way. By such means the Roman Catholic institutions of Lower Canada become immensely rich.[73]

Cartier's rising income allowed him to indulge his inherited bourgeois tastes. In its simplest form this meant attention to comfort, food, furnaces, carpets, and gas-lighting. However, Montrealers of Cartier's rank sought more than storm windows, a full stomach, and a large house. The perception of Cartier by English Canadians as an unaggressive French-Canadian *bon vivant* obscured his serious social ambitions that are attested to by his wine cellar, servants, library, and hotel bills, by his stable, fruit trees, and country estate, by his military commission, baronetcy, coat of arms, uniforms, and hair style.

Cartier accumulated a large amount of furniture and moveable goods in his three residences and law office. Although his widow was given most of his silverware, nine chandeliers, jewellery, and other valuable personal items, his moveable effects sold for $5,123 (table 5). His homes contained few paintings or valuable works of art although as previously mentioned he did buy a marble bust in Naples and paid $435 to have it shipped to Montreal.[74] Music was important to Cartier. He liked to sing and dance and encouraged his daughters to play the piano well. Pianos were expensive and an important sign of status; only 9 per cent of bourgeois homes in France contained any musical instrument and, because of their cost, pianos were particularly rare. Cartier had two pianos and rented one for his daughters when they were abroad for extended periods.[75]

An impressive wine cellar was always a mark of prestige and as early as 1853 Cartier bought madeira by the cask and cognac by the gallon. In his early years he liked the Richelieu Valley concoction of rum, sugar, and warm water; later he was known for his taste in champagne.[76] When he died he left eleven cases of wine in one residence, 240 bottles of claret, four cases of champagne and ten cases of wine in Ottawa, and a barrel of sherry, a barrel of Bordeaux, four cases of champagne, and a case of brandy at his country home.[77]

Despite his public disdain for "bookish" learning, Cartier's own library was auctioned in January 1875 for the considerable sum of $1,843 of which $826 came from the sale of his law books, $591 from his government publications, and $163 from books, pamphlets, and

Cartier and his daughters Hortense and Josephine,
Dorchester Street, Montreal

Cartier, Maurice Cuvillier, and three priests, 1867

brochures on Canada.[78] Over half of the $263 received for the balance of his books which formed his personal collection came from the sale of his French encyclopedia, Gustave de Beaumont's history of Ireland, and back copies of the *Illustrated London News* and the *Eclectic Magazine* (figure 4).

The library's monetary value should not be inflated since the law books formed a special "professional" category and the holding of government documents and Canadian works was probably in large part the result of free distribution to government ministers. Nor can one ascertain how many of his books were received as gifts or were part of his ménage with Luce Cuvillier. Finally, it is impossible to know which books Cartier actually read. Although his broad-based conservatism embraced fundamental questions of property, monarchy, law, and education, Cartier avoided theory and even encouraged a certain anti-intellectualism in his audiences. Reading, he often pointed out, was of little use in the marketplace or political arena.[79]

Comparisons cannot be made with the holdings of his Canadian peers but his library did have much in common with Parisian bourgeois of the same period. Like his European counterparts he bought erotic travel books on the Orient and Egypt; his library also reflected the vogue for dictionaries and encyclopedias as well as the interest in practical guides—*Essai sur l'art d'être heureux, Cuisinier Parisien, Cartes à jouer*, several books on oratory, a Spanish reader, an Italian grammar, and an itinerary of Paris (figure 5).[80] Although it included neither Burke nor Locke his library was strongest in eighteenth- and nineteenth-century political theorists and historians like Voltaire, Rousseau, Montesquieu, Chateaubriand, Lammenais, Tocqueville, Bagehot, Mill, Macaulay, Bancroft, Hamilton, and Marshall. The presence of authors like Proudhon, Ricardo, and Bères (*Les classes ouvrières*) implies that Cartier was aware of class questions. For a man who liked music, his library contained surprisingly few works on music or art, although there are indications that his wife removed some books of this description, or at least the sheet music from his country home.[81] He owned works by major Catholic philosophers like Veuillot, Bossuet, and Pascal, one work on the papacy, and three copies of Muslim's *Les Saints Lieux*, but like his Parisian peers he had no devotional literature. His fascination with the peerage, heraldry, and other trappings of nobility is clearly reflected in his library. On the other hand there is no evidence of a literary interest in the military, if one ignores eleven copies, presumably complimentary, of a pamphlet entitled *On the Art of Operating under Enemy Fire*.

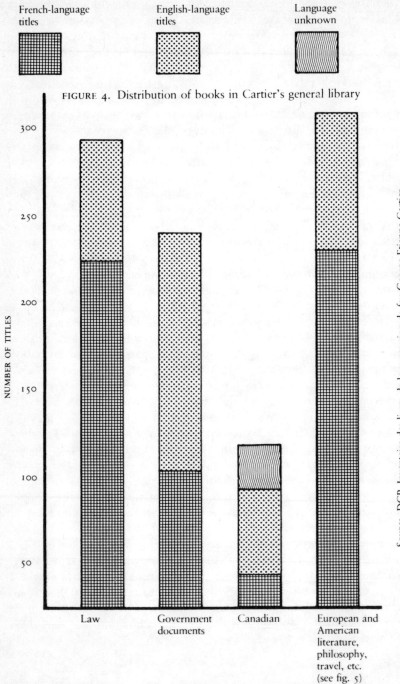

FIGURE 4. Distribution of books in Cartier's general library

Source: DCP, Inventaire des livres de la succession de feu George-Etienne Cartier.

Cartier's lighter reading was almost entirely in French and included such contemporary authors as Balzac, Dumas, Hugo, George Sand, and Eugène Sue. His interest in the theatre is witnessed by the seventy-nine volumes of the *Répertoire du theâtre français* and twelve volumes of Voltaire's plays. The only exceptions to his preference for French literature were English copies of Longfellow's *Hiawatha* and Stowe's *Uncle Tom's Cabin*, and a large collection of English periodicals.[82] The government, Canadian, and to a lesser extent law publications reflect a professional pull towards English as a working language (figure 4).

Luce Cuvillier stimulated Cartier's interest in country life, riding, and viticulture. In September 1869 he bought a 122-acre farm at Longue Point on the eastern outskirts of Montreal.[83] Located in a favoured area for the country homes of Montreal's élite, Cartier's farm was just a few estates away from the Symes's "Elmwood" and the Cuvilliers' "Review Cottage." Cartier named his home "Limoilou" after Jacques Cartier's village in Brittany. Fronting on the St. Lawrence the property had a large vegetable garden, a vineyard, orchard, pasture, cultivated fields, and a small creek. The main house, a stone dwelling, was built towards the river and had a parlour, livingroom, and five bedrooms. A smaller frame house, barn, and silo located closer to the toll road to Montreal were leased. Particularly interested in fruit trees, Luce had Cartier's gardener buy apple, plum, peach, and cherry seedlings from the finest American nurseries. It was at Limoilou that Cartier kept the family piano, his pony, his popular novels, and his twelve-year collection of the *Illustrated London News*.[84]

Cartier's comfort and isolation from daily problems were assured by a hierarchy of friends, associates, hired help, and servants. Law clerks and junior partners handled the routine of his law practice; his political secretaries—L. W. Sicotte and later Benjamin Sulte—protected him from office-seekers and trouble-makers. Important investment matters were supervised by Maurice Cuvillier, the country estate was managed by Luce Cuvillier, minor banking was dealt with by his valet. The Cartiers always had help for the domestic duties of cleaning, washing, cooking, household repairs, gardening, child care, vehicle maintenance, and shopping. Cartier had both a housekeeper and a part-time waiter in Ottawa, a groundskeeper and seasonal farm labourers at the country estate, a handyman for maintenance of his urban properties, at least three servants in his wife's residence, and when needed, a driver and cab hired on a monthly basis.[85]

For at least five years Cartier had a valet. Although it necessitated two hotel rooms, Thomas Vincent travelled with Cartier, was privy to his private life, and a witness to his death. In addition to the usual concerns

FIGURE 5. Distribution of books in Cartier's personal library

English-language titles

French-language titles

Source: DCP, Inventaire des livres de la succession de feu George-Etienne Cartier.

Note: For law, government documents, and Canadian books, see fig. 4.

of a manservant—boots, shaving, wardrobe, cabs, errands—Vincent handled Cartier's petty finances; he cashed cheques, paid bills, bought stamps, advanced money to Cartier, and kept a petty cash book. With Vincent in attendance Cartier had little need for cash. Although active almost until the day he died, Cartier left in his room only three £5 notes and some small change.[86]

Cartier always enjoyed travel and good hotels—the Hotel Bedford and Grand Hotel (Paris), Brevoort House (New York), Hotel de Rome (Naples), Adelphi Hotel (Liverpool), and his favourite, the Westminster Palace Hotel in London. The Cartiers, together or separately, travelled in a style that befitted their rank. Despite generous luggage allowances, Lady Cartier and her daughters paid a surcharge for surplus baggage on one European trip. They dined at the captain's table and Hortense was invited to smoke a cigarette in the captain's private quarters.[87] En route to London in 1866 Cartier hired a wagon as well as a carriage to transport his luggage from his New York hotel to the steamer. The luggage included a silk-lined accessory bag, a monogrammed tooth-brush kit, a looking glass, soap box, nail brush, ink box, instrument board, and individual cases for his playing cards, combs, and brushes.[88]

Although he visited other major European centres—Paris, Rome, and Geneva—London was Cartier's first love. His fascination with British life dated from at least the 1850s. In 1853 he named his daughter Reine-Victoria. A year later he began subscribing to the *Illustrated London News* and by the end of his life subscribed to ten British periodicals, none from France. He visited London for the first time with the Canadian delegation of 1858. After 1865 he was in London, often for months at a time, in every year except 1871. His tendency to dally in England angered French-Canadian nationalists, amused his friends, annoyed his cabinet colleagues, and interfered with his ministerial and political functions. "Sir George tarde trop," Hector Langevin complained on one occasion. "Je suis obligé d'organiser toute la milice en son absence."[89] While other Canadian politicians wilted on the London social circuit, Cartier thrived, accepting up to five invitations a day to garden parties, teas, official dinners, and country visits. He bought the London *Times' Etiquette for Ladies and Gentlemen* and read four British newspapers a day when staying at the Westminster Palace Hotel. Rumours that Cartier would stay in London as plenipotentiary of Canada or as attaché to the colonial secretary were encouraged by Cartier himself: "If tomorrow I had the means, and could get myself out of this maelstrom of politics I might be tempted to settle myself in London."[90]

Fully aware of Cartier's political utility and status in the Canadian colony, the British also enjoyed his spontaneity and salon charm. They found no contradiction between the punctilio displayed in his purchase of tights and black stockings to meet the Queen and his lack of inhibition in singing a French-Canadian solo for the Prince of Wales or in arranging guests in make-believe canoes on a parlour floor for the singing of riverboat songs.[91] A gallic anglophile or, as he described himself, "a French-speaking Englishman," he impressed the British as a pre-Revolution French gentleman, "un gentilhomme du temps de Louis XIV conservé dans les traditions canadiennes."[92] He conversed in French at Lambeth Palace with the Archbishop of Canterbury, stayed at Windsor Castle with the Queen, dined regularly with Lord Carnarvon, and had tea with the Duchess of Wellington. He liked dining at the Conservative Club and, with Governor General Monck's sponsorship, was given temporary membership in the Athenaeum Club. Longstanding professional contacts with British businessmen involved in Canadian commerce led to visits to the homes of George Glyn and Sir Morton and Lady Peto. During his final stay in 1872–73, Cartier was integrated into the community of Montrealers living in London—the Roses, Molsons, Stephens, and Brydges. In January 1873 the Roses entertained Cartier and fifteen other guests, all Canadian, at lunch.[93] Much less influenced by French society, he did receive an invitation to meet Prince Napoleon at Versailles.

By the 1860s Cartier was an anglophile in his clothing tastes and, according to his daughter, "always bought his things in London." These included balmoral boots, goatskin gloves, calling cards, "18 super linen collars 'marking G. E. Cartier'," "8 rich silk Windsors," "3 enamel and pearl waistcoat buttons," "13 pair of Gold collar studs," "perfume and lavender water," and "a gold folding handframe and 2 pair of blued steel turnpin frame spectacles." His hairstyle reflected his changing ambitions and by 1868 he was regularly visiting a London hairdresser to have his hair washed, puffed, powdered, "carded and made into tail." In 1869 he visited a wigmaker.[94]

Cartier had a lifelong attraction to pomp, military structures, orderly organization, and uniforms; his behaviour, both in a public and in a family context, was autocratic. It was Cartier who organized the St. Jean Baptiste Society in the 1840s on the model of the Roman legion with *centurions, décuries,* and *dizaines*. His unabashed love of uniforms surprised even members of the British aristocracy. "Mr. Cartier," wrote Governor General Monck's niece, "dined in full uniform! No one knows why."[95] Thirty years after graduating he pleased school officials by appearing at a Collège de Montréal commencement in full school uniform. In 1868 he had Bennett and Company, London military outfitters, alter his dress uniform and clean the gold lace. While in the shop he bought silk stockings and a morning-coat with a silk waist-band.

Cartier's attention to rank is clear from his indignation that John A. Macdonald had been knighted while he had been given the lesser title of Companion of the Bath. If he was posturing when he complained that French Canadians felt "deeply wounded" that their "representative man" had a lesser title, his anger can be explained by his desire for British social status.[96] For years he had bought books on the peerage and when finally created a baronet in 1868 Cartier carefully supervised the creation of his coat of arms: "It would not be possible to remove the gold from the flags without destroying the drawings, but if Sir George would write upon the back of the drawing he sends to England that he wishes ermine spots upon the flags instead of the fleur-de-lys, it would suit the purpose intended."[97]

Service as an officer in the Canadian militia was a traditional form of status for the francophone élite. As we have seen, Cartier's grandfather had aided the British in the American Revolution and had become a lieutenant-colonel in the Verchères militia. Cartier's father had served as a lieutenant and paymaster in the War of 1812. In 1847 Cartier himself, just ten years after being charged with treason, was appointed a captain in the Montreal Voltigeurs militia unit. He established the Ministry of Militia Affairs in 1861 and chose militia as his portfolio after Confederation. In 1862 his government was defeated over his expensive, thirty-six-page militia bill. In resigning Cartier explained that his only desire was that Canadians should play a full role under the British flag. The next major (though abortive) attempt to reorganize the Canadian military was in 1868 when Cartier presented a bill calling for military schools, a navy, conscription in certain cases, and an active militia of 40,000 men.[98]

Military status and rank only in part explain Cartier's enthusiasm. In addition to its defensive role, the military had important ideological and institutional functions in aiding commerce and in enforcing authority in Canadian society. He was convinced that "the commercial spirit" followed the British army. In practical terms, the garrison was always an important market for the Montreal business community; Cartier himself had rented one of his largest buildings as a military hospital. As the British military presence in Canada declined, Cartier called for increased military expenditures that would give "additional security" to British capitalists and ensure "cheaper" capital in the future. Military force was also an integral part of the authority structure, essential for what Cartier called "the completion of national greatness": "J'ai déjà fait observer, en d'autres circonstances, que trois éléments indispensables constituent une nation, une population, le territoire et la marine. Mais le couronnement, indispensable aussi, de l'édifice, est la force militaire."[99]

Cartier's admiration for Victorian England, its status symbols, its parliamentary system, its military structures, its social contract between aristocrats and commoners, and its perceived commitment to progress, individualism, and industrialism did not exempt him from the value systems of his French-speaking peers. In France "les anglomanes" of the industrial period inherited a rich eighteenth-century pro-English tradition from "philosophes" such as Montesquieu. Prominent French capitalists like Jules Siegfried touted "anglo-saxonism" as a counter-force to France's radicalism and instability. Anglophilism was also respectable among the French-Canadian bourgeoisie; the studies of Yvan Lamonde, for example, have shown the significant British inspiration in francophone cultural activity in Montreal.[100] Like the English Canadians of a later generation portrayed by Carl Berger, Cartier and many of his peers seem to have sought legitimacy and security in British values and institutions. Threatened by French, American, and native radicalism, they used "Britishness" to control their adversaries and to guarantee their social position. This ideological alliance was cemented by economic ties, titles, travel, language, and military service. As an urban landlord Cartier had the British military for a tenant, as a lawyer his most important client was a British-owned railway. He became an officer in the militia, minister of the crown, and a baronet.

Cartier's business career, family life, and social attitudes do not correspond to the interpretations of French Canada expounded by sociologists like Everett Hughes and Horace Miner nor to the models projected by national Catholic historians like Lionel Groulx. Cartier's family life and marriage were far from exemplary. Living apart from his parents after the age of ten, he resided in a school dormitory and hotels for at least eighteen years. His first daughter was born while he and his wife inhabited Montreal's finest hotel. In the last years of his life communications with his wife were often handled by his business partner. Separated from her husband, Lady Cartier devoted herself to preparing her daughters for marriage, the very institution which had led to her embitterment. The diaries of the two girls make clear that they were aware of this paradox and yet both were apparently trapped by their sex and class. Cartier's daughters seem typical of "la jeune fille

Cartier's birthplace, "House of Seven Chimneys," St. Antoine-sur-Richelieu, Que.

OTHER EXAMPLES OF BOURGEOIS HOUSING: *opposite above*, Cartier's country house, "Limoilou," Longue Pointe, Que., 1914; *below*, Cartier's town house, 32 Notre Dame Street, 1885; *above*, Lady Cartier's villa, Cannes, France (purchased after Cartier's death)

bourgeoise" who, in Roland Barthes' words, "produisait inutilement, bêtement, pour elle-même."[101] They rejected their father and his lifestyle and yet complained of empty lives devoted to masses, piano lessons, and social activities oriented to finding them a "gentleman." Neither ever married, entered a convent, or led an independent professional life.

For his part, Cartier preferred the company of Luce Cuvillier. It is as though Luce, his music, and his country estate enabled him to escape the very Montreal world he was helping to shape. Behind the frenetic pace, the materialism, and the titles, one senses in Cartier a confirmation of Flaubert's aphorism that "chaque notaire porte en soi les débris d'un poète."[102]

Although the Cartier-Cuvillier relationship violated the norms expected of a French-Canadian Catholic husband and father, there was no public outcry. It is intriguing that his opponents attacked political and religious deviance in Cartier but never exploited his vulnerable private life. This may have been part of an unwritten nineteenth-century political code. The Toronto *Globe*, as noted, was quick to distort the Catholicism of Cartier's concubine and her influence on her rich Protestant niece but went no further. For its part, Montreal bourgeois society—its newspapers, religious leaders, and social institutions—adapted to Cartier's personal circumstances and protected him.[103]

Chapter Three
Working Politician

The Union period (1841–67) was a watershed for the Montreal bourgeoisie. Their region's orientation changed from Papineau, toryism, separatism, furs, and seigneuralism to La Fontaine–Cartier conservatism, federalism, steam, and restructured social and economic institutions. At the same time, centrifugal forces weakened traditional loyalties. Responsible government and the dismantling of British mercantilism threatened important elements in the English-speaking community. Overpopulation and emigration worried the French-Canadian élite while business spokesmen chafed at the inaptitude of Quebec's educational, legal, and landholding structures to new market and worksite conditions.

Urbanization and industrialization brought opportunity, wealth, and employment; they also entailed poverty, overburdened institutions, and ethnic, religious, and class tensions. Irish Catholics battled their French coreligionists, the Sulpicians sparred with the bishop, the division between the right and the left in the francophone bourgeoisie intensified, and young entrepreneurs exploiting new forms of transportation and production challenged older merchants. Changing trade patterns, fluctuating immigration, and American jingoism brought added pressures. As the city spread west along the Lachine Canal, eastward towards Hochelaga, and north to the flanks of the mountain, ethnic and class enclaves were accentuated. Ethnic relations in Montreal were always fragile. A cholera epidemic, election demagoguery, a religious festival, or heightened unemployment often signalled outbreaks of violence. At another level, ethnic hostility formed an integral part of class conflict, metropolitan competition, the struggle between different entrepreneurial groups, and the rural-urban confrontation.

The francophone bourgeoisie of Montreal was particularly vulnerable in the post-rebellion period. Prime instigators of the events of 1837–38, its members saw their movement broken and their political rights suspended. Papineau made his way to France, Ludger Duvernay launched a newspaper in Vermont, Robert Nelson went to California, his brother was exiled to Bermuda, and Denis-Benjamin Viger languished in a Montreal jail. Aggressive and condescending, the Durham Report sharply delineated the future of French Canada. The Union Act reunified the St. Lawrence economic unit, denied responsible government, and gave the Lower Canadian majority only equal representation in the united assembly. The appointment of Charles Poulett Thomson, a businessman and former cabinet minister, as governor, and his overbearing political tactics, added to the insecurity. Despair was a common reaction. There remains no joy or idealism, wrote one *patriote*, only the isolation of one class from another; Montreal was "an offensive morgue."[1] Few *patriotes* sustained the idealism expressed by Chevalier de Lorimier in a letter written to Cartier hours before going to the gallows:

> Prison de Montréal
> 12 février 1839
> 9 heures du soir

Mon cher Cartier,

Il ne me reste plus qu'à préparer ma conscience pour un autre monde et à faire mes adieux à mes amis. Il en coûte toujours à laisser ce monde quand des liens aussi forts que ceux qui m'unissent à la terre existent, mais pas autant qu'on se l'imagine lorsque la mort se montre dans le lointain. Plus on la considère de près, moins elle est dure, moins elle est cruelle. Si beaucoup la redoutent autant, c'est parce qu'ils n'ont pas pensé sérieusement à mourir. Pour ma part, cher Cartier, je suis dévoué, ferme et résolu. Je remercie le Ciel de me donner autant de force. Je n'ai pas voulu entreprendre le voyage long de l'éternité sans t'adresser mes remerciements sincères pour tes services nombreux que tu m'as rendus et t'assurer de mes sentiments de gratitude et d'amitié que j'entretiens envers toi.

Puisse le ciel t'accorder une longue et heureuse carrière. Puisses-tu prospérer comme tu le mérites et te rappeler que je suis mort sur l'échaffaud pour mon pays. Adieu ---

> Ton sincère et dévoué ami
> Chevalier de Lorimier[2]

Never one to despair in the search for first causes, Cartier rebounded from the rebellions as an early proponent of compromise with British authorities. Although living in a *patriote* milieu in Burlington, Vermont, he did not participate in the second wave of rebellions that persisted through 1838 and, as we have seen, officially abandoned the *patriote* cause in the declaration he sent to Lord Durham's secretary in September 1838. Pleading that the treason charge against him was "imméritée," he stated his willingness to post a bond guaranteeing fulfilment of "mes devoirs de citoyen et de sujet britannique." A personal letter written two days later confirmed the sincerity of his official declaration.[3] When the treason charge was dropped Cartier returned to Montreal. Still fearful of arrest, he remained in hiding for two months, not resuming his law practice until early in 1839. His full reintegration into official society was signalled by his presence at the governor's levée, November 6, 1839.[4]

Cartier maintained this sensitivity to the reality of British power. Convinced that "l'Angleterre pouvait gouverner comme elle le voulait," he refused to support La Fontaine in opposing the implementation of the Union Act.[5] Within a few years of the rebellions he was interpreting his participation in the events of 1837 not as an act aimed at "separation" from Britain but as one motivated by opposition to "an oppressive minority"—the Lower Canadian tories.[6]

It was Louis-Hippolyte La Fontaine who gave form to what would become the dominant political ideology of Quebec. Seven years Cartier's senior, a lieutenant of Papineau, and a moderate, he had sought a middle ground even before the rebellions and by 1839 had found a viable compromise in which he could work both sides of the street as a "successor of Papineau and a disciple of the British constitution."[7] While opposing the Union Act he would—once it was imposed—work within its terms to achieve power.

La Fontaine abandoned Papineau's ruralism, idealism, and dreams of independence for a program based on responsible government, economic development, and new pragmatic political alignments. A changed attitude to English Canadians was inherent in his leadership. The Union Act's reservation of forty-two seats for Upper Canada and the same for Lower Canada meant that power would almost inevitably fall to a party with a base in both ethnic groups. A careful nose for useful English-speaking allies, an adherence to British constitutional practices, a search for political and institutional separateness within the developing federal system, assiduous use of patronage in the construction of the Quebec Conservative party, isolation of liberal nationalists, and maintenance of a French-Canadian bloc were elements of La Fontaine's legacy to Cartier.[8]

Quickly identified as La Fontaine's aide-de-camp, Cartier knew of his leader's secret negotiations with Francis Hincks in 1840 and in the same year he joined Hincks, Lewis Drummond, Viger, Berthelot, and William Walker for discussions at La Fontaine's house.[9] Although refusing to run for an assembly seat in 1841 and 1844, he organized elections for Reform candidates in the Montreal region and even during his father's final illness he helped La Fontaine in the important Terrebonne campaign. Pleased with La Fontaine's appointment to the cabinet in September 1842, he promised to toast the new attorney general with champagne. In September 1844 he spoke in St. Denis. Seven years before, he reminded voters, he had joined the villagers in firing on British soldiers. Now it was their duty to reject Denis-Benjamin Viger's nationalism in favour of responsible government.[10]

By the late 1840s the La Fontaine conservatives' alliance with prominent members of the clergy and English-speaking reformers, and the acquisition of responsible government, assured them of an important share of political power. This prospect combined with Cartier's long political apprenticeship, his marriage into an important Montreal family, and his sizeable legal and real-estate income to make elected office a logical direction for his career. In April 1848 he ran as Reform candidate in a by-election in Verchères, a riding with sentimental associations for the Cartier family and a relatively safe Reform seat. Cartier had been born in the riding and his grandfather had represented it (1805−9). Campaigning on responsible government, temperance, and his family roots in the riding he was elected with a 248-vote majority. His victory celebration included a banquet in the seigneury house of Varennes and a parade replete with flags, rifle salutes, and 100 horsemen.[11]

Cartier remained a member of the assembly of the United Canadas until Confederation (table 6). He sat for Verchères until 1863 and for Montreal-East, 1863−67. After 1867 he exercised a double mandate, sitting in both the federal House of Commons and the Legislative Assembly of Quebec. While he was elected easily in Verchères, the Montreal elections—with the exception of that of 1863—were hard-fought. Despite his well-organized and lavishly financed campaigns, Montreal voters rejected him in 1857, 1861, and again in 1872. Although he won with a good margin, the 1867 election, marked by the combined tensions of Confederation and a working-class opponent, was particularly bitter and violent.

On Jaunary 18, 1849, Cartier walked through the Montreal snow to

TABLE 6

Elections

DATE	COUNTY	CANDIDATES	VOTES CAST	%
		(* - victor)		
April 1848 (by-election)	Verchères	Amable Marion Cartier*	552 738	42.8 57.2
April 1851	Verchères	acclamation		
June 1854	Verchères	— Massue Cartier*	614 804	43.3 56.7
Feb. 1855 (by-election)	Verchères	Christophe Préfontaine Cartier*	1,060 1,246	46 54
Dec. 1857	Verchères	Christophe Préfontaine Cartier*	elected	
Dec. 1857	Montreal (3 seats)	A.A. Dorion* D'Arcy McGee* John Rose* Luther Holton Henry Starnes Cartier	4,332 4,301 4,192 4,103 4,028 3,670	17.59 17.46 17.02 16.66 16.37 14.90
July 1861	Montreal-East	A.A. Dorion* Cartier	1,527 1,502	50.4 49.6
July 1861	Verchères	Cartier*	elected	
June 1863	Montreal-East	A.A. Dorion Cartier*	1,203 1,879	39 61
April 1864 (by-election)	Montreal-East	acclamation		
Sept. 1867	Montreal-East (federal)	Médéric Lanctot Cartier*	2,085 2,433	46.1 53.9
Sept. 1867	Montreal-East (provincial)	Ludger Labelle Cartier*	2,051 2,408	46 54
July 1871	Beauharnois (provincial)	Célestin Bergevin Cartier*	324 750	30.2 69.8
Aug. 1872	Montreal-East (federal)	Louis-Amable Jetté* Cartier	3,264 2,007	61.9 38.1
Sept. 1872	Provencher, Man. (federal)	acclamation		

Sources: Normand Séguin, "L'opposition canadienne-francaise aux elections de 1867 dans la grande région de Montréal" (M.A. thesis, University of Ottawa, 1968) p.59; Brian Young, "The Defeat of George-Etienne Cartier in Montreal-East in 1872," *Canadian Historical Review* 51 (December 1970): 404; Best thesis, pp.89, 129, 143, 170, 549; and *La Minerve*, April 6, 1848, August 1, 1854, December 23, 24, 1857, July 6, 1871, June 11, 1863.

the nearby legislative buildings in St. Anne's market and began his twenty-three-year parliamentary career. Scattered around the assembly were his colleagues of the next few decades. A fellow Montrealer, Lewis Drummond, was in his seat as was Quebec City's aggressive Joseph Cauchon and Sherbrooke's Alexander Galt. Glengarry had sent John Sandfield Macdonald and Kingston a quiet young lawyer named John A. Macdonald.

With Papineau in the assembly, rebellion losses on the order paper, and annexation in the wind, the member for Verchères at first attracted little attention. He was, however, tough, impatient, and often rude, and soon displayed an ambitiousness that grated. As John A. Macdonald put it, he could not show himself "superior to office." Lady Macdonald thought he was "extremely egotistical."[12] Cartier was a short man of five feet six inches, and disdaining exercise he tended to paunchiness. Observers noted that his head and small hands were constantly moving. He brushed his thick, dark hair straight back and sported mutton-chop whiskers as a young man. In his later years his eyes bothered him or "wanted rest," as he told John A. Macdonald, and he purchased spectacles in London. A fastidious dresser, he wore the silk hat, bow tie, and wide collar of the day and a small golden figure of Napoleon.[13]

As a politician, Cartier delegated administrative responsibility effectively, was an excellent committee debater, and thrived in political backrooms. He was never a good public speaker and observers agreed that a Cartier speech was rambling and dull, his high-pitched voice unpleasant, his English weak, his French undistinguished. Journalists found his speeches "disagreeable in the extreme" and remarkable only for their length. Cartier's lifetime achievement, according to one critic, was a drill shed and 2,000 "horrible, incomprehensible, untranslatable and unrepeatable speeches."[14]

Despite these defects, Cartier's political star rose rapidly. A party organizer and backbencher in 1849, he dominated Montreal politics by the mid-1850s. La Fontaine, describing himself as "tired" and "disgusted" with political life, resigned in 1851 and moved to the bench. This brought to power Cartier's cousin by marriage, Augustin-Norbert Morin.[15] Cartier was soon asked to enter the Hincks-Morin cabinet as solicitor general but refused, telling Morin that for financial reasons he wanted to continue practising law. A year later he gave the same reason, plus his opposition to the government's acceptance of the principle of an elected legislative council, for declining the public works portfolio.[16] This refusal to join the Hincks-Morin government was probably a wise tactical decision. In 1853 Hincks was implicated in a well-publicized scandal while in Quebec the ministry was weakened by the attacks of Cauchon on the right and L. V. Sicotte and Luther Holton on the left. The government was quickly defeated at the outset of the 1854 session and an election was called for June 22.

This election came at a particularly hectic time for Cartier and illustrates the pressures to which he was subjected. Since Morin was a weak campaigner, it was Cartier who acted as chief Reform organizer in Quebec. Accusing the Rouges of destructiveness and ridiculing their alliance with the Grits, his newspaper *La Minerve* linked the Rouges to European socialists. The election campaign was only part of his responsibility. As president of the St. Jean Baptiste Society he had to preside over the annual celebration which came just two days after the election. Nor were election conditions particularly favourable to the government party. The mayoralty election in February 1854 in which Cartier had campaigned against his father-in-law had left fresh wounds and in the late spring cholera again infested Montreal. City newspapers carried the names of up to twenty victims a day, many of them children. As the symptoms of diarrhea and vomiting spread, civic leaders had no solution but to urge citizens to be abstemious and to drink mint tea.[17] Within two weeks of Cartier's re-election in Verchères, his daughter and father-in-law were both dead from the epidemic.

Between 1854 and 1857 Cartier moved closer to the centre of the stage. His nomination as speaker at the outset of the session of 1854 proved to be the finale for the Hincks-Morin administration. At a joint caucus the Grits and Rouges agreed to oppose him. Upper Canadians attacked his Grand Trunk sympathies; in Lower Canada he was unpopular with liberals like John Young and conservatives like Joseph Cauchon. Cartier received only 23 of 42 French-Canadian votes and was defeated 69 to 59. In January 1855, however, he was named to his first cabinet post as provincial secretary in the MacNab-Taché government.[18] The office was particularly appealing since the provincial secretary had inherited many of the functions of the governor general's secretary, notably the task of processing civil service applications.

In May 1856 Cartier became attorney general for Canada East, a post which, with the exception of a few days out of office during the double shuffle in 1858 and two years in opposition, 1862–64, he retained until Confederation. As the most important French Canadian in the first post-Confederation ministry, he took militia and defence as his portfolio. Another indication of his political power was his alliance with John A. Macdonald, Conservative leader and attorney general for

Canada West. When Sir Etienne-Paschal Taché resigned as co-premier late in 1857 the first Macdonald-Cartier ministry was formed. Despite some vicissitudes Macdonald and Cartier collaborated until the latter's death in 1873.

TABLE 7

Some political offices held by or offered to Cartier

OFFICE	DATE
Member, Legislative Assembly of United Canadas	1848−67
Member, House of Commons, Canada	1867-August 28, 1872; Sept. 14, 1872−May 20,1873
Member, Legislative Assembly, Quebec	1867−73
Declines office of Solicitor General	Nov. 1851
Declines office of Commissioner of Public Works	Sept. 1852
Defeated as candidate for Speaker of Assembly	Sept. 1854
Provincial Secretary	Jan. 27, 1855−May 24, 1856
Attorney General (Canada East)	May 24, 1856−July 30, 1858
Inspector General	Aug. 6−7, 1858 (double shuffle)
Attorney General (Canada East)	Aug. 7, 1858−May 31, 1862
Attorney General (Canada East)	March 1864−June 1867
Declines office of Chief Justice[1]	April 1866
Minister of Militia and Defence, Canada	July 1867−May 1873

1. ANQ, Chapais Collection, Box 7, N. Belleau to Cartier, April 12, 1866.

This access to the top rung of the Canadian political hierarchy—signified by a seat in the cabinet, coalition with leading Ontario Conservatives, missions to England, titles, and company directorships—was predicated on Cartier's ability to deliver power in Quebec, and more particularly in the Montreal region. His aggressiveness, pragmatism, worldliness, and urban conservatism suited Montreal's changing mood. The middle-class violence of 1837 and 1849 had given way to political standpatism and a concern for concrete economic issues like reciprocity, railways, and harbour development.

Rapid economic development characterized Montreal in the Union period. Bustling, commercial, and chaotic, Montreal was still twice the size of Toronto. The city's population grew 56 per cent in the decade 1851−61 and another 19 per cent from 1861 to 1871; the census of 1871 reported a population of 107,225.[19] In 1854 the Grand Trunk Railway opened its shops in Point St. Charles. In the thirty years before Confederation, sixty manufacturers located along the Lachine Canal. Shipbuilders like Brush, McDougall, and Gilbert, and iron industries like the Montreal Rolling Mills, and the Montreal Rolling Stock Company all benefited from Montreal's position as the hub of Canadian transportation development. New companies specializing in nails, scythes, axes, and various lead, copper, and rubber products flourished alongside older shoemaking, tanning, and brewing industries. The city's sewing-machine industry employed 1,500 workers by 1872.[20]

While the diverse elements of Montreal's middle class settled down to building careers and homes, political and social control over the city's heterogeneous elements—as evidenced by Cartier's own election experience—remained tenuous. The riot of June 1853 ignited by the visit to Montreal of Alexandre Gavazzi was typical of the religious and social unrest that the city's élite was unable to control. Since the assembly was in session, Cartier was probably in Quebec City when the ex-monk's harangue against Roman Catholics brought the Irish into the streets and left ten dead. Cartier kept a low profile and was not named to the jury of important citizens who examined the affair. A transient population, cholera epidemics, and ethnic and religious tensions emphasized Montreal's essential disorder. Housing was inadequate and the population density almost doubled in twenty years from 11,195 people per square mile in 1851 to 20,800 in 1871.[21] Fuel shortages occurred, that of the winter of 1872 being particularly severe. Despite rapid improvement in the Quebec literacy rate in the Union period, illiteracy in Montreal remained high.[22] Women, children, immigrants, and other unskilled workers formed a cheap labour pool for the city's expanding industries. In 1871, for example, the shoemaking industry in Montreal employed 1,915 women and 664 children under the age of sixteen.[23]

At the core of Cartier's strength was his cementing of the alliance between Montreal's francophone bourgeoisie and the wealthy, gallican wing of the Roman Catholic Church.[24] A third source of power was the increasing support Cartier received from the English-speaking élite of Montreal. Less tory and less isolated from the French-speaking business community than their elders, young entrepreneurs like Alexander Galt, John Rose, and J. J. C. Abbott found an obvious ally in Cartier. He was more commercially oriented than La Fontaine, more flexible than Langevin, and more stable than Cauchon. Nor was he an ethnic threat. As early as 1843 Cartier had rejected strident French-Canadian nationalism as well as Durham's argument for the assimilation of French Canada. Canada, he argued, was in a "happy situation" and "blessed by providence" to have two great civilizations within its bosom. Both ethnic groups could benefit from the philosophy, history, and literature of the other. English-speaking Montrealers were assured that French Canadians had British hearts and were committed to the happiness and prosperity of Canada.[25] An inveterate defender of Quebec's English-speaking minority, he displayed an easy-going catholicism and was socially acceptable at prominent events such as the St. James Club ball. His English steadily improved and in the mid-1860s the governor general's sister-in-law was surprised to find that Cartier "always speaks English."[26] On important issues such as the abolition of seigneurial tenure, the recodification of civil law, and economic development Cartier spoke for the Montreal business community.

Despite the drama of annexation and rebellion losses Cartier's first session saw the passage of important measures concerning canals, railways, postal services, and municipalities. Whatever their ethnic and religious differences, politicians agreed on the benefits of economic growth. With this consensus, economic bills were often an unspectacular part of the session in which members in a club-like atmosphere promoted the growth of their favourite enterprise.[27] Only later when the Grand Trunk's bleeding of the public purse became spectacular was strong opposition raised. In 1849 the assembly unanimously passed Francis Hincks's Guarantee Act, a bill with more long-term significance for the taxpayer than the Rebellion Losses Bill. Guaranteeing 6 per cent interest on one-half the cost of any railway over seventy-five miles in length, it accelerated the public largesse to railways. Much of the important work concerning company law, regional trade-offs, and subsidy programs was handled by legislative committees. In 1852 Cartier became chairman of the all-important railway committee, a position he held until Confederation.

Charters were an essential part of every session's business. They gave companies or institutions monopolies, tax concessions, land grants, exemptions from restrictive laws, or direct cash subsidies. Located at the core of the St. Lawrence system, Montreal's politicians sponsored charters for a wide range of companies that included transcontinental railway and suburban streetcar operations, banks, manure producers, and benevolent associations.

Besides his well-known activities on behalf of the Grand Trunk Railway (see chap. 4), Cartier was always diligent in his responsibilities to individual companies. Early in his parliamentary career he sponsored petitions on behalf of the St. Lawrence and Atlantic Railway and John Rose's British American Mining Association. When the Mutual Insurance Company began defaulting on claims arising out of the Montreal fire of 1852, Cartier introduced a bill to save it from bankruptcy.[28] In

1860 he argued strongly for increasing the subsidy of Hugh Allan's Montreal Ocean Steamship Company to £104,000. If Allan's weekly steamship service to Europe was not heavily supported by the Canadian government, he declared, it would be "ruiné" by competition from companies subsidized by the British and American governments. Seven years later Cartier did his best to reassure depositors that the bankrupt and soon-to-disappear Commercial Bank "was solvent beyond doubt."[29]

More important than his action on behalf of individual companies was Cartier's role in the systematic organization and integration of Quebec's institutional, social, and legal structures. This new framework was needed to facilitate the subsidization of transportation enterprises and to aid the accumulation and disposition of new forms of public and private capital. Cartier also assisted in the formulation of a public opinion that would legitimize the changing nature of work in Montreal's emerging industrial society and rationalize the state's positive role in this transformation. He was an enthusiastic supporter of the Great Exhibition of 1851 in London's Crystal Palace and encouraged local industrial expositions that would stimulate a favourable climate for business in Quebec.[30] During the 1840s and 1850s municipal and ecclesiastical bodies were reorganized and given corporate status, including the right to borrow and to invest in certain situations; it was Cartier who introduced the Municipal Act of 1860. Regulations concerning bills of exchange, mortgages, and interest rates were of direct concern to the commercial community. Convinced that a six-day period of grace for promissory notes impeded commerce, Cartier helped Protestant and Roman Catholic banking institutions settle on a special arrangement that halved the period of grace and yet took Catholic holidays into account.[31] Quebec mortgage law was reorganized by a bill presented by Cartier in 1860. This law was of particular importance to creditors since it permitted mortgages to be registered only after presentation of a certificate-of-title for the property to be mortgaged.[32] In 1853 interest rates had been fixed by the assembly at 6 per cent. Five years later, Cartier—despite the opposition of local farmers—was one of the few Quebec members who supported a measure which retained the maximum 6 per cent interest rate on bank deposits but permitted banks to lend at 7 per cent.[33] During the agricultural depression of 1860 he opposed attempts to abolish the 1858 rates. Cartier also attacked a bill that would have forced insurance companies to open their books to closer public scrutiny.[34]

While all Montreal politicians advocated transportation development, Cartier distinguished himself by his tireless promotion of any communication scheme that might serve the Montreal business community—a transatlantic telegraph cable, a bridge over the St. Lawrence, harbour improvement, dredging the St. Lawrence ship-channel, improving navigation in the Richelieu River, toll-free canals. In 1849, while his Montreal peers furiously debated the question of annexation to the United States, Cartier visited upstate New York to discuss canal and steamboat connections between the St. Lawrence and Lake Champlain. For two terms he sat on the Montreal Harbour Commission, an important body which supervised port development, channel improvements, bridge sites, and harbour access. He publicly supported six different railways that would serve Montreal—the St. Lawrence and Atlantic Railway(1846), the Montreal and Prescott Railway (1850), the Quebec and Halifax Railway (1852), the Grand Trunk (1853), the Intercolonial Railway (1864), and the Canada Central (1870).[35]

These efforts were appreciated by entrepreneurs and by the 1860s even the once hostile Montreal *Gazette* had kind words for Cartier, the "liberal and tried friend of the British population of Lower Canada."[36] Hugh Allan's lawyer justified large campaign contributions to Cartier on the grounds that "On every one of these subjects—steamships, railways, canals—the Government had a policy which was favourable to his [Allan's] views, and in my opinion three times the sum would have been well spent if it had been necessary to keep a Government in power

TABLE 8

Directorships

SECTOR	COMPANY	OFFICE	DATE
Banking and loan	Montreal City and District Savings Bank	Director	1846
	Canada Loan Company	Director	1853
Insurance	National Loan Fund Life Assurance Society of London	Director	1847
	Canada Life Assurance Company	Director	1849
	British North American branch of Life Association of Scotland	Director	1863
Transportation	Montreal and Kingston Railway	Provisional director	1851
	Grand Trunk Railway	Provisional director	Nov. 1852–May 1853
	Transatlantic Telegraph Company	Director	1858
Mining	Montreal Mining Company	Director	1856, 1863, 1871

which had according to his views, and my own too, the improvement of the country so deeply at heart as this Government appeared to."[37] Banking, insurance, transportation, and mining companies named Cartier to their boards; their owners financed his election campaigns, directed legal work to his office, invited him for weekends at their country estates, and provided free train tickets for his family (table 8).

Cartier's espousal of economic expansion did not extend to enterprises that were antithetical to Montreal's development, for although he spoke as a French-Canadian *chef* his real bailiwick was Montreal. In 1853 John Young proposed a canal to facilitate steam traffic between the St. Lawrence and Lake Champlain. Fearing a diversion of traffic from Montreal, Cartier was blunt. Unless the canal terminus was placed directly opposite Montreal, he would vote against the bill.[38] Quebec City, a local victim of the transformation to steel, steam, and railways, received little help from Cartier. In 1849, while the panic-stricken Quebec City Board of Trade pointed out that the abolition of the Navigation Acts was a death-knell for the region's traditional trade, Cartier preached free trade. His advocacy of the Grand Trunk Railway, American markets, and improvements in the St. Lawrence ship canal, and his preference for Ottawa as capital, were hostile to the old capital's traditional administrative role and its interest in overseas markets and the square-timber trade.[39] The perennial difficulties of the North Shore Railway in obtaining financial support from the Macdonald-Cartier administrations are further proof of his perspective as a Montrealer and Grand Trunk lawyer rather than of an ethnic or nationalist economic outlook.[40]

The Cartier Conservatives depended on support from traditional Quebec and—although his income was increasingly drawn from urban sources, the interests he defended were urban, and he himself had lived in Montreal from the age of ten—references in a Cartier speech to a French Canadian and his farm were an essential ritual. In his first speech in the assembly Cartier emphasized the importance of the grain trade for French Canadians and the fact that he himself still cultivated crops, presumably on the St. Antoine homestead. The more he grubbed in Montreal politics the more romantic and abstract became his concept of French Canada. Speaking over Ludger Duvernay's grave in Côte des Neiges cemetery, Cartier paid tribute to this "intimate and indissoluble" union of the French Canadian and the soil.[41] In another speech he described farm ownership, blood, and language as the foundation of the French-Canadian heritage: "L'attachement au sol, c'est le secret de la grandeur future du peuple canadien-français. On parle beaucoup de

nationalité. Eh bien, je vous le dis, la race qui l'emportera dans l'avenir
c'est celle qui aura su conserver le sol. . . . Attachez-vous donc à la terre,
travaillez la avec amour." [42] Once his rural credentials were established,
Cartier progressed to urban themes. In his maiden speech it was the call
for railway construction. To expand the markets for Quebec grains,
Canadians should subsidize railways joining Montreal to Portland,
Boston, and New York.

Like most francophone representatives of rural counties around
Montreal, Cartier's real base was urban. In Montreal, Cartier cultivated ties with his bourgeois peers through professional and associa-
tional activities, as a patron of the Société Historique, director of the
City and District Savings Bank, president of the Advocate Library of
Montreal, president of the St. Jean Baptiste Society, captain in the
Montreal Voltigeurs militia unit, and member of the organizing committee for the Paris Exposition of 1854–55, and the examining board
of the Montreal Bar Association. He made financial contributions to
the local reading-room and for years presided over a section of the St.
Jean Baptiste Society that included La Fontaine, Gédéon Ouimet,
Henry Judah, and John Pratt. His *dizaine*, or ten-member cell in the
society, consisted of six lawyers, a merchant, a clerk, a notary, and a
dentist.[43] Schools for the francophone élite received special attention.
He endorsed construction of the Jesuits' Collège Sainte-Marie and gave
out prizes at the Villa Maria Convent. Twice he attended graduation
exercises at his alma mater, the Collège de Montréal.

This exposure and linkage to his local peer group was an important
source of political feedback. In the spring of 1857 the Montreal Bar
Association met to discuss judicial reorganization. Hostile to Cartier's
proposed bill in this regard, the association petitioned him to delay the
legislation. Cartier's law partner, Joseph-Amable Berthelot, was on the
select committee formed to discuss the bill; his future law partner,
François Pominville, was secretary of the association. Before the petition reached him officially, Cartier had received three reports and a
handwritten copy of the minutes. Besides Berthelot and Pominville, two
other Conservative lawyers sent reports of the meeting to their "cher
ami."[44]

Cartier's interest in temperance, burial, and fraternal societies, savings banks, and fire protection show his awareness of working-class
malaise, the city's endemic cultural instability, and the general problem
of urban social control. Cartier appeared at the firemen's ball and was a
member of the Repeal Association of Ireland.[45] He supported the new
Côte des Neiges cemetery; his close friend C. A. Leblanc was vice-

president of the temperance society. After the disastrous east-end fire of July 1852 Cartier contributed £25, attended a rally in Bonsecours Market, and was named to the aid committee.[46] For future fire protection he proposed improvements in the city's water supply, the banning of inflammable roofs, and the widening of city streets. In 1854 he was elected president of the St. Jean Baptiste Society and led the annual parade. After this event, which was temporarily interrupted when the typographers' float—bearing a working printing-press—lost a wheel, Cartier went on to take communion with Mme. La Fontaine and preside over a banquet at the St. Nicholas Hotel. His speech emphasized the need for French-Canadian unity and paid careful tribute to all elements of society—the temperance groups, the press, firemen, students, and the Institut Canadien.[47]

Cartier's local power was accentuated by the division in his party between the Montreal and Quebec City sections. By the mid-1840s the Reform party had two distinct wings. La Fontaine permitted Joseph Cauchon and his Quebec City allies to control local newspapers, patronage, and the party warchest.[48] Responsibility for the Montreal region was delegated to Drummond and was ultimately inherited by Cartier. The existence of regional independence rather than horizontal integration within the Conservative party in Quebec gave Cartier great influence over local affairs, especially since the Union Act reinforced central control over municipal, educational, and judicial institutions.

Although he did not actually represent a city riding until 1863, Cartier's position in the party gave him political power at all levels in Montreal—ranging from nominating an alderman in 1849 and a Montreal harbour commissioner in 1866 to presenting the 1860 bill to divide Montreal into three ridings. He delegated control of the Conservative slush fund in Montreal to Henry Starnes, president of the Board of Trade and director of the Richelieu Navigation Company, the Montreal Warehousing Company, the Metropolitan Bank, and the Montreal City and District Savings Bank. Cartier called Starnes one of the most "indispensable" Montreal Conservatives.[49]

An urban lawyer who spoke primarily for commercial interests, Cartier sat until 1863 for the rural riding of Verchères where his family assured him of a strong network of legal, clerical, and business contacts. His brother wrote to him concerning local educational and constituency problems. Another brother and cousin served as parish delegates on the Verchères county council; a brother-in-law ran for the Conservatives in neighbouring Bagot county; a distant relative, Eusèbe Cartier, was named legislative councillor for St. Hyacinthe in 1855. The family's

standing in the Richelieu Valley was strengthened by the marriage of
two of his sisters to local doctors. His third sister was a prominent
member of the riding set.[50]

In Verchères a politician's round included temperance meetings,
funerals, and ploughing matches. Cartier also attended weddings, sat
on the organizing committee of the Provincial Exhibition of Agriculture
and Industry, and subscribed to the *Agricultural Journal and Transactions of the Lower Canada Agricultural Society*.[51] Party newspapers
like *La Minerve* voiced concern for agricultural problems and printed
letters from rural constituents. Cartier was always willing to help a local
clergyman with a political problem. In 1863, for example, the Bishop of
St. Hyacinthe asked him to sponsor the incorporation of the diocese's
caisse ecclesiatique.[52] This attentiveness to the needs of the clergy was
repaid during elections when local priests often served as virtual campaign organizers for Conservatives. Cartier never hesitated to call on
clerical allies. In the elections of 1863 he warned Curé Labelle that
Protestants were observing the morality of Catholic priests and would
be shocked if Labelle supported the "scandalous" behaviour of the
opposition candidate. He wrote to a curé in the Drummond-
Arthabaska riding asking him to straighten out problems in the Conservative camp and to remove one of the candidates.[53]

Cartier's election campaigns were characterized by irregularities,
violence, payoffs, and coercion. In the 1840s he managed Lewis
Drummond's campaigns and learned the mechanics of bilingual meetings, torchlight parades, Irish dockers, and free whiskey. The 1844
campaign against William Molson was particularly vicious. Both sides
were armed and fights broke out at election meetings in Griffintown,
the Haymarket, and Place d'Armes. Drummond's agents brought Irish
canalworkers from Lachine and distributed them to the polls: one
Molson worker was knocked unconscious, stripped, and wakened to
"find himself naked except his legs."[54] On the second day of voting the
Riot Act was read and, despite Cartier's opposition, fifty soldiers were
sent to disperse the crowd in the Haymarket. In the mêlée that followed
a Drummond supporter died of bayonet wounds.[55] As Drummond's
lawyer and polling agent at the Haymarket, Cartier played an active
role at the inquest, charging that "murder" had been committed against
a "peaceable citizen." The villain, according to Cartier, was the magis-
trate who had unnecessarily called in the troops.[56] Cartier squabbled
with the coroner and disrupted the inquest by cross-examining witnes-
ses even though the jury objected to any participation by lawyers; the

lieutenant in command of the troops refused to answer his questions. Despite Cartier's efforts, the jury concluded that the victim had died of a "misadventure."[57]

Growing political stature in the 1850s did not change Cartier's election tactics. In 1854 he defended the right of Timothy Brodeur to take his seat as the representative of Bagot. Acting as both returning officer and candidate, Brodeur had declared himself elected by acclamation. Cartier responded to charges of tyranny in the matter by accusing the opposition of violating parliamentary tradition out of "pure curiosity."[58] Four years later he tried to avoid receiving a corruption charge by leaving alone at his home a servant who was too young to receive a supoena. This case was finally dismissed on a technicality.[59] The coercion and manipulation of voters by physical force, cash payment, drink, or intimidation by employers was routine in Montreal, particularly before the introduction of the secret ballot. One campaign official told Cartier that he had received only 100 votes in 1872 from the riding's 1,000 shoemakers because "nous n'avions pas de quoi payer leurs ouvriers." According to the opposition press, Cartier workers paid $10 a vote in 1867; Cartier was reputed to have said that Irish voters could be bought for a "barrel of flour apiece and some salt fish thrown in for the leaders."[60] Rhetoric aside, there is no doubt that Cartier's election campaigns were carefully managed. Jean-Louis Beaudry—returning officer in Montreal-East in 1867, president of the Banque du Peuple, ex-mayor of Montreal, and a Cartier supporter—arranged polling stations and voting lists to suit the government. His brother, a gas-company executive, threatened his employees with dismissal unless they voted for Cartier.[61] One month after the election Beaudry was named to the Legislative Council of Quebec. In recommending his appointment Cartier explained that he owed his election to the Beaudrys: "Par leur fortune, leurs propriétés et leur influence commerciale dans ma division, ils constituent un élément de la plus haute importance."[62]

The added tension of a working-class candidate in 1867 and a nationalist opponent in 1872 made the last campaigns of Cartier's career particularly turbulent. Rotten eggs, free beer, and husky dockworkers made public meetings almost impossible. On election day in 1872 forty provincial police were sent into Montreal-East in response to rumours that "bullies" supporting Cartier would be opposed by "cabaleurs" armed with pistols. In fact election day was relatively quiet; campaign workers for the opposition were given pepper-shakers rather than pistols. The only disturbance occurred when a well-known tavern-keeper, Joe Beef, discharged "a splendid volley" in the direction of Cartier partisans.[63]

Newspapers were essential ingredients in Quebec campaigns. Often functioning as auxiliaries of a political party, they printed party platforms, announced rallies, and denounced the opposition as traitors or communist demagogues. To ensure a suitable orientation, papers such as the Montreal *Gazette* were bought outright by entrepreneurs. Two other Montreal newspapers, *Le Nouveau Monde* and *Les Mélanges religieux*, were sponsored in part by the Bishop of Montreal.[64] Other papers depended on government advertising or political handouts. Cartier's law office bought space for legal announcements in two Montreal newspapers.[65]

La Minerve was Cartier's house organ in Montreal. After a lengthy exile in Vermont, its proprietor, Ludger Duvernay, reestablished the paper and by 1843 it was a strong Reform supporter. Cartier and Duvernay patched up their personal relations and in 1843 *La Minerve* supported Cartier's election in Verchères. For the rest of his career *La Minerve* defended him—discreetly concerning corruption or disquieting features of his private life, vociferously in building his image as *chef* and in attacking Rouge, Grit, and ultramontanist opponents.

Patronage was the glue of local party power. Although Confederation lent idealism to his acts, Cartier was always a tough infighter, party organizer, and patronage-broker with a clear idea of what most people wanted in politics. A generation before being implicated in the Pacific scandal, Cartier was being attacked as crass, corrupt, destructive, brutal—a "Walpole moins le talent."[66] Twenty years ago, *Le Pays* noted in 1858, Cartier was a "patriote enragé" involved in all the "isms" of his day: "now he believes in nothing except conquest and spoils."[67] Nor was he attacked just by his opponents. The French consul in Canada reported that corruptness was the greatest fault of the Cartier régime.[68]

As early as the 1850s all administrative decisions in the Montreal region, and appointments of judges, militia officers, customs officials, school inspectors, and even prison chaplains, crossed Cartier's desk. Sheriffs, aldermen, militia inspectors, and ward officials filtered information to his office. A fellow cabinet minister agreed to a request from a local curé for changes in the St. Jérôme mail service but only "par l'entremise de Cartier."[69] When a Beauharnois politician complained that his recommendations for a judgeship had been ignored, Cartier briskly replied that patronage was a government responsibility. In

Verchères he cancelled the mail contract of a Rouge; in another village he used a technicality to oust an opponent as mayor.[70] Beneficiaries of government patronage were expected to follow the party line. Cartier was particularly incensed at the independence shown by a lawyer named by the government to prosecute unlicensed taverns.[71]

The Montreal Post Office was notorious for heavyhanded patronage. Cartier had placed so many supporters in the post office, according to the *Gazette*, that the postmaster "did not know what to do with them."[72] Cartier's nominations of judges and Queen's counsels were another source of rancour. A. A. Dorion described one Queen's Counsel appointee as a "known swindler," another was a "scoundrel," and a third was a "forger who had escaped from this country to avoid the penitentiary."[73] Two Montreal judges were described by another opposition member as "men out of their heads; others were men of bad moral character, and another was so deaf that in a case where a man sued for $10 the judge gave judgment for $100."[74] Nonplussed by these attacks Cartier retorted that "some of the best decisions given by a most eminent Judge had been delivered when he was totally blind."[75] As the minister of militia Cartier had at his disposal a large budget, construction contracts, and appointments. A priest from Three Rivers suggested to Cartier that the government could ease the diocese's financial problems and repay Bishop Laflèche for his election help by buying the Seminary of Nicolet for use as a military institution.[76] In May 1868 Cartier presented a $4,000,000 bill to provide fortifications "for the defense of Montreal and other cities." While Cartier justified the expense as a means of showing a Canadian commitment to Great Britain, the opposition dismissed the bill as simple pork-barreling in his own backyard. The militia, they charged, was topheavy in overpaid officers; his department was "more lavish of silver than it would ever be of lead in the defense of the Dominion."[77]

These examples emphasize that patronage was an intensely partisan act—a reward for service rendered, recognition of a family connection, or neutralization of a potential opponent. At the same time the nomination of a judge, the choice of a county seat, or the raising of a regiment were important political and social acts. *Fonctionnarisme* was more than just a way of rewarding friends: government jobs—or the hope thereof—helped stabilize society and Cartier never forgot La Fontaine's emphasis on patronage as one means of entrenching the francophone bourgeoisie.[78] The widening scope of government activity in Montreal offered potential employment to all levels of society and small communities around Montreal understood the effect on local economics of the presence of a courthouse, customs house, or provincial police station. Cartier's judicial decentralization bill (1857) with its provision for new judges, nineteen county seats, and the construction of jails and court houses brought windfall political dividends. St. Christophe, a small village in Arthabaska, held a special meeting to thank Cartier for naming it as county seat.[79] Berthier County was less pleased at being placed in the judicial district of Sorel on the other side of the St. Lawrence. "And I cannot but reflect here," D. M. Armstrong reminded Cartier, "on the fact that ever since the present party has been in power, the Representatives of the County of Berthier, have, through good report and evil report, unflinchingly supported their party and I must remark that our friends are truly not rewarding such a faithful adherence with a fair return."[80]

The vulnerability of their Rouge opponents was another source of strength for the La Fontaine-Cartier Conservatives in the 1840s and 1850s. Rouge support in 1849 for annexation to the United States, their long bruising battle with the bishop over the Institut Canadien, and their incongruous alliance with the Ontario Grits made them easy marks for charges of radicalism and anticlericalism. By the 1860s, however, the disparate Rouge, Liberal, and nationalist elements were settling down into a moderate political party capable of capitalizing on French-Canadian nationalism, worker unrest, anti-Confederation sentiment, the gallican-ultramontane struggle, or hostility to Cartier's political tactics. Liberals like Honoré Mercier and Louis Jetté were pragmatic urban politicians who understood ward politics, patronage, and the need for English-speaking allies in Montreal. By the late 1850s they were joining forces with powerful businessmen like Luther Holton and John Young.[81] While the Rouge newspaper *Le Pays* continued to joust with the bishop over Italian unification, the editors of the moderate *L'Ordre* sought coexistence with the ultramontane clergy. One hundred and thirty-five moderates bowed to clerical pressure in 1858 and abandoned the Institut Canadien. While challenging Cartier on nationalist and liberal political issues, the Liberals shared the Conservatives' expansive economic program and accepted St. Lawrence capitalism as a fact of life. Their program in 1872 included improved St. Lawrence communications and support for the Pacific Railway.[82]

Cartier's aggressive Conservative leadership grated on the Rouges as did his apparent betrayal of both his *patriote* origins and his marriage into a Rouge family. A favourite Rouge target, Cartier never hesitated to respond in kind. Criticized by his former *patriote* mentor in 1841, Cartier reacted by accusing Duvernay of "malice" and "indiscretion" and by sending him a three-year-old legal bill.[83] In the elections of 1844 he attacked the Viger nationalists head-on. Privately he accused them of "errors," "unjust calamities," and "venomous tongues"; publicly he ridiculed their obsession with the past, their negativeness, and their misreading of the meaning of the rebellions.[84] Industry and progress, according to Cartier, could only be achieved by a positive attitude, responsible government, and a coalition with Ontario reformers.

This mutual hostility soon escalated into physical violence. At a heated political meeting in the Hotel Nelson in June 1844, a nationalist lawyer struck Cartier after the latter called him "impertinent." Later that evening Cartier named a second and sent the lawyer, Guillaume Lévesque, a note demanding justice for the "grave and offensive" insult. A duel was only avoided when Lévesque signed an apology drawn up by Cartier.[85] In 1848 the Rouge newspaper *L'Avenir* questioned Cartier's performance at the battle of St. Denis. Cartier went straight to the newspaper offices and demanded an apology. Although the articles had not been written by him, it was the pugnacious Joseph Doutre who took up Cartier's challenge. After one site was abandoned because of police intervention, a duel was held in Chambly. Shots were exchanged but neither Cartier nor Doutre were hit.[86]

The Montreal municipal elections of 1854 were a particular embarrassment for Cartier since his father-in-law, E. R. Fabre, was Rouge candidate for mayor against Cartier's friend and fellow Conservative, Dr. Wolfred Nelson. *La Minerve*, which spoke for Cartier, urged Fabre to restrict himself to the "gentle joys" of his family and bookstore. Instead of Fabre's brand of unstable, Papineau-inspired nationalism, it called for a law-and-order administration and settlement of the city's immigrant and transient problem. Nelson's victory ensured further Rouge efforts to unseat Cartier that culminated in his defeat in Montreal-East in 1872.[87]

This vendetta-like atmosphere had roots not only in Cartier's abrasive personality and his party's ability to monopolize power. Ideologically, the Rouges and later the Liberals opposed Cartier's unrelenting and systematic political conservatism. While they also spoke for factions in the bourgeoisie they felt that Cartier exaggerated in his efforts to protect property, the propertied class, and the hierarchical structures which protected these privileges. An anathema to many nationalists and yet a logical conclusion of his conservatism was Cartier's praise for the conquest, which had "saved us from the misery and the shame of the French Revolution. The conquest ended by giving us the fine and free institutions which we possess today, and under which we live happy and prosperous."[88] Cartier often returned to the theme that, like French-Canadian nationalism, property was threatened by foreign ideologies: "un écrivain [Proudhon] dans un moment de délire, a osé proclamer que la propriété, c'est le vol. . . . Maxime blasphématoire et délétère."[89] Given this threat to property—"l'élément qui doit gouverner le monde"—Cartier wanted to ensure that the state was not overthrown by popular elements: "nous voulons prendre les moyens d'empêcher la tourmente populaire de jamais bouleverser l'état."[90]

Cartier's political conservatism included support for an established church, insistence on age and property as necessary conditions for public office, admiration for the evolutionary characteristics of the British parliamentary system, and distrust of American political institutions. An enthusiastic monarchist, he opposed frequent elections, the secret ballot, and universal suffrage.[91] Before 1864 Cartier was a perennial opponent of representation by population, attacking it as too democratic, as a prelude to universal suffrage, and as a form of Upper Canadian tyranny. Nor, he argued, would his Montreal-area constituents gain by the transfer of political power to Upper Canada inherent in representation by population. Although admitting that this concept formed part of British constitutional practice, he emphasized that the mother country carefully balanced it against the interests of property and social class. He insisted that he would oppose the implementation of a system of representation by population even if Quebec had a larger population than Ontario.[92]

Throughout his career Cartier objected to attempts to increase remuneration for members of the assembly, arguing that longer sessions would be the only result. Indeed, Cartier proposed the outright abolition of payment for elected representatives, a measure which would have further restricted representation to wealthy individuals.[93] In 1856 the opposition tried to assure the independence of the assembly by obliging members to resign their seats if they received other government remuneration. The measure, for example, would have prevented a member being hired by the crown to plead a government court case. Cartier opposed this measure on the ground that a member should be free to serve his country in as many capacities as possible.[94]

After the formation of a federal structure in 1867, Cartier favoured the double mandate which permitted the holding of a provincial and a federal seat at the same time. The exercise of the double mandate by Cartier and five other prominent Quebec Conservatives (Premier Chauveau, Joseph Cauchon, Hector Langevin, John Jones Ross, and Christopher Dunkin) was a factor in the systematic subordination of the Quebec government to Ottawa in the years after Confederation. Cartier, for example, sat on three committees of the provincial assembly, including the committee on railways, canals, telegraph lines, and mining and manufacturing corporations. At the same time he acted as chairman of the House of Commons' railway committee.[95]

As well as trying to restrict the number of voters, their choice of candidates, and conditions of voting, Cartier endeavoured to protect appointed and executive authority from encroachment by elected officials. This is clear from his persistent efforts to retain an appointed upper house as representative of property. He cited his opposition to the government's plan to concede an elected legislative council as one reason for not entering the Hincks-Morin cabinet in 1852. Men should gain money and experience first; after the age of thirty-five those who could meet stiff property qualifications could sit in the upper house.[96] His proposal for a £2,000 ($8,000) property qualification for membership in the legislative council was extremely high.[97] At Confederation Cartier was a strong advocate of a bicameral system for Quebec. An upper house in which members had life appointments, he argued, would serve to supervise the popular and potentially unstable lower branch of the legislature. He envisaged his duty as that of protecting Quebec's strong "conservative" and "monarchical" traditions by enveloping "nos institutions politiques de tout ce qui peut contribuer à leur stabilité."[98]

The annexation movement of 1849, the debate over the choice of a capital, and Confederation provided three opportunities for the exercise of Cartier's political conservatism and his use of British institutions as a guarantee of the status quo and as a bulwark against popular unrest.

Annexation further split the Montreal bourgeoisie, a social group already deeply divided by the Rebellion Losses Bill and the subsequent burning of the legislature. During the summer of 1849 many of Montreal's English-speaking élite signed a manifesto calling for annexation to the United States. Among the petitioners who proclaimed the bankruptcy of the British connection and the St. Lawrence commercial empire were John Redpath, John Torrance, John Rose, Luther Holton, John Abbott, and John Molson. On Cartier's left, important Rouges like Joseph Doutre and the Dorion brothers argued that a French-Canadian state was possible within the American union. Friends like Alexander Galt and John Donegani shared Cartier's economic viewpoint but opted for annexation; *La Minerve*, usually faithful to La

Fontaine, supported republicanism. Cartier's father-in-law based his
1850 Montreal mayoralty campaign on annexation and was elected
along with an annexationist city council.

Cartier himself never wavered in opposing annexation. As a
homeowner, real-estate developer, and captain in the Montreal militia,
the status quo suited him. His law practice was flourishing, his directorships increasing, and he could anticipate political power under the
Union Act. His allies, the railway entrepreneurs, were free-traders
largely untouched by the collapse of British mercantilism. Another
factor in his opposition to annexation was his lifelong distrust of
American democracy, its radicalism, and its "absence d'une personnifi-
cation de l'autorité exécutive qui impose le respect à tous."[99] Cartier
saw little relationship between trade and loyalty. Expanded rail links
with the United States, and reciprocity were possible without political
annexation. This was a major theme of his first speech in the assembly
and in June 1849 he participated in a free trade rally in Montreal. He
voted for the Rebellion Losses Bill and after the burning of the legislature he and Drummond organized a petition of loyalty which they
personally presented to the governor.[100]

In October 1849 he and sixteen legislators, mostly from the Montreal
region, countered the annexation manifesto with another petition in
favour of law and order and British institutions. The petitioners clearly
feared social unrest and the "agitation" from which "the city has
suffered so much" and which had as its result "the upheaval of the
social order and the renewal of the troubles and commotions of which
we have already deplored the disastrous results."[101]

Choosing a permanent capital was another issue that bared the
inherent instability of the united Canadas, divided Quebec by exacer-
bating metropolitan tensions, and showed the continuing strong fear of
urban unrest in Montreal among leaders like Cartier.

After the burning of the legislative buildings in Montreal, the
capital—despite the opposition of Cartier and other Montreal-area
politicians—rotated between Toronto and Quebec City. The "nomadic
system," as one newspaper called it, was costly and inconvenient.[102]
Upper Canadians felt isolated in Quebec City; French Canadians disliked Toronto. Transportation to both cities was difficult. In the early
1850s Cartier usually travelled to Quebec City by steamer. Before
completion of the Grand Trunk, one Montreal lobbyist spent five
winter days journeying via Albany, Niagara Falls, and Hamilton to visit
Cartier in Toronto.

Montreal's tradition of lawlessness, the events of 1849, and the city's vulnerability to American attack largely eliminated it as a serious contender. Many Montrealers themselves were not sure that they wanted the capital. However, Montreal-area representatives consistently voted for a fixed, as opposed to rotating, site.[103] Given Upper and Lower Canadian tensions, the only possible sites were in the Montreal-Ottawa-Kingston triangle. As early as 1855 Cartier voted for a fixed capital but called for an open vote that would not tear the ministry apart. He attacked the costs of an alternating capital and produced statistics showing construction costs of £300,000 for a permanent parliament that would include an art gallery and a museum of fine arts.[104] Costs, however, were not the issue. Essential for administrative reasons, the selection of a permanent capital created a political impasse. The endless manoeuvring in the spring of 1856 featured a thirty-hour debate, charges by George Brown that the French-Canadian members were "insolent," and ultimately the resignation of ministers.[105]

While expressing token support for a motion that Montreal be chosen because of "its central position," Cartier preferred Ottawa as capital. It was within Montreal's orbit and yet isolated from the city's turbulence. Cartier reminded Montrealers that it was their own "surexcitation" in 1849 that had cost them the seat of government. Ottawa did not have a francophone majority but was predominantly Roman Catholic. While observers such as the governor general felt that the choice of Ottawa was a means of facilitating English-speaking domination of Canada, Cartier chose to emphasize that the development of Ottawa would encourage French-Canadian colonization in the Ottawa Valley. Above all, he favoured Ottawa because it was isolated from public pressure—"la pression de l'opinion publique se fera moins sentir là qu'ailleurs."[106]

In 1856 Quebec City was chosen capital but Upper Canadian members voted down construction funds; the confusion was compounded when the Legislative Council threw out the assembly's bill.[107] Out of this chaos came the first Macdonald-Cartier ministry which in 1857 submitted the issue to the Queen. The Colonial Office's choice of Ottawa, the Macdonald-Cartier government's defeat over the issue in July 1858, the double-shuffle, and the return of the Conservatives only confused matters. Finally, in February 1859, Cartier and Macdonald made the choice of Ottawa a party vote. Although one Montreal-area politician resigned from the cabinet and fifteen Quebec members broke government ranks, Ottawa was chosen by a majority of five votes.[108] The political capital, as Cartier wished, would be remote from Montreal mobs.

Confederation resulted from chronic political stalemate. By 1859 the assembly had voted over 200 times on the seat-of-government issue and every session was poisoned by interminable debates over the question and over various schemes to introduce representation by population.[109] Political paralysis was everywhere evident. Cartier's own political career stalled and after seven years in power he spent two years in opposition, 1862−64. In addition, the economy was sluggish, the United States was bellicose, and Britain's changing colonial policy had made her increasingly reluctant to meet heavy Canadian costs.

Federalism was one solution for politicians seeking economic expansion, social stability, and a resolution of the political crisis. It was also a logical extension of political and administrative forms developed under the Union Act. Cartier, however, accepted the judgment of his peers only slowly.[110] Well before his acceptance of the principle of federal union, fellow Lower Canadian politicians like Joseph-Charles Taché, Joseph Cauchon, A. A. Dorion, D'Arcy McGee, and Alexander Morris had begun to legitimize the idea. A sarcastic critic of Alexander Galt's federal union proposals before the summer of 1858, Cartier did an about-face with the collapse of the short-lived Brown-Dorion government.[111] Named prime minister in August 1858, Cartier brought Galt into the cabinet by accepting the principle of federation. Two months later he was in London with Galt and John Ross to discuss federation at the Colonial Office, and although the document was apparently Galt's work, Cartier's name was prominently attached to the federation proposal.[112]

In 1864, following George Brown's initiative before the constitutional committee and the emotional meetings on the floor of the assembly and in Quebec City's Hotel Saint-Louis, Cartier joined the coalition cabinet committed to federalism and representation by population. Although it was George Brown who made the significant gesture, it may have been Cartier's region that made the more important concessions. The application of proportional representation in the all-important House of Commons as opposed to an ongoing structure of equal provincial representation or a double-majority system facilitated the integration of Quebec francophones into a larger English-speaking state. For their part, the province's anglophones were relegated to a minority position within Quebec by the implementation of a federal system.

On several occasions Cartier explained why he had accepted representation by population and minority status for French Canadians—principles which he had fought for years. He had, of course, other explanations than George Brown's interpretation that Cartier had been cornered "by the compulsion of circumstances" and "driven into the necessity of taking up the representation question openly and vigorously."[113] Whereas Brown predicted to his wife that French Canadianism would be "entirely extinguished," Cartier argued that French Canada would be protected by representation by population in a federal state.[114] *La Minerve* discerned a difference between its application under the existing union and in the proposed federation. Under the former it would bring "servitude and degradation" but applied in a larger federal union, representation by population would be "a safeguard and guarantee of independence."[115] The difference would result from the addition of the Maritimes which, according to Cartier, would offset any threat from Upper Canada:

> In a struggle between two—one a weak, and the other a strong party—the weaker could not but be overcome; but if three parties were concerned, the stronger would not have the same advantage; as when it was seen by the third that there was too much strength on one side, the third would club with the weaker combatant to resist the big fighter. He did not oppose the principle of representation by population from an unwillingness to do justice to Upper Canada. He took this ground, however, that when justice was done to Upper Canada, it was his duty to see that no injustice was done to Lower Canada. He did not entertain the slightest apprehension that Lower Canada's rights were in the least jeopardized by the provision that in the General Legislature the French Canadians of Lower Canada would have a smaller number of representatives than all the other origins combined.[116]

Usually a tenacious *quid pro quo* bargainer, Cartier apparently demanded little in the federation negotiations at Charlottetown and Quebec City in the autumn of 1864; unlike Galt and other defenders of special-interest groups he did not fight hard on specific issues.[117] Protection of sectional interests was largely delegated to an upper house that did not exercise financial control and whose members were named for life by the central government. According to Cartier this upper house, the Senate, would be "our security."[118] Provincial autonomy was also compromised by the granting of the appointment of the lieutenant governor to the central government. Even more threatening to many francophones and defenders of provincial rights was the federal power of disallowance. However, as a centralist Cartier accepted a broad and vague definition of disallowance envisaging its use in cases of what he called "unjust or unwise legislation."

Outside Quebec, Cartier's behaviour in 1864 was interpreted as a symbol of ethnic cooperation. He received standing ovations before English-speaking audiences when he sang "God Save the Queen" in French, visitors to the Quebec Conference praised his graciousness, and his gallic charm was welcome in London drawing-rooms. Observers were particularly impressed by his call for ethnic harmony and a new "political nationality":

> Now, when we were united together, if union were attained, we would form a political nationality with which neither the national origin, nor the religion of any individual, would interfere. . . . We were of different races, not for the purpose of warring against each other, but in order to compete and emulate for the general welfare. We could not do away with the distinctions of race. We could not legislate for the disappearance of the French Canadians from American soil, but British and French Canadians alike could appreciate and understand their position relative to each other. They were placed like great families beside each other, and their contact produced a healthy spirit of emulation.[119]

Speaking throughout the Maritimes after the Charlottetown Conference Cartier expressed fears common to many British North Americans. Reiterating his distrust of American democracy, he argued that Confederation would give Canada a distinctive "monarchical element." The alternatives were simple: "either we must obtain British American Confederation or be absorbed in an American Confederation."[120] Cartier also regularly reminded audiences of their common commercial interests. "Prosperity" was the word he repeated in his Maritimes speeches.[121] Federation would lead to the abolition of customs barriers and to the building of the Intercolonial Railway joining Quebec to the Maritimes.

Within Quebec, critics focused more on provincial autonomy and minority rights than on ethnic cooperation. Christopher Dunkin and A. A. Dorion pointed out the possibility of indiscriminate disallowance and the potential tyranny of an overlapping party system. Dunkin felt that French Canadians—given the lopsided nature of Confederation—would be able to retain power only by being aggressive. Dorion spoke in favour of what he called a "real Confederation" in which the important powers were put in sole jurisdiction of the provinces. Identifying Cartier as a conservative who wanted to strengthen the power of the crown and diminish the influence of the people, Dorion described the proposed federation as "the most illiberal constitution ever heard of in any country where constitutional government prevails."[122] His outspoken brother was even blunter. Accusing French Canadians of being "fast asleep," he charged that Confederation would be simply "Legislative Union in disguise" and provincial legislation "nothing but a farce."[123]

Angry opponents of Confederation in Quebec derided Cartier as a tyrant, monarchist, spokesman for railway interests, and the dupe of Upper Canadians who would "throw him aside like a worn-out towel":

> To attain this eminence, he has crushed the weak, cajoled the strong, deceived the credulous, bought up the venal, and exalted the ambitious; by turns he has called in the accents of religion and stimulated the clamor of interest—he has gained his end. . . . When his scheme of Confederation became public, a feeling of uneasiness pervaded all minds; that instinct forewarned them of the danger which impended. He has hushed that feeling to a sleep of profound security. I shall compare him to a man who has gained the unbounded confidence of the public, who takes advantage of it to set up a Savings Bank. . . . When that man has gathered all into his strong box, he finds an opportunity to purchase at the cost of all he holds in trust, the article on which he has long set his ambitious eye; and he buys it, unhesitatingly, without a thought of the wretches who are doomed to ruin by his conduct. The deposit committed to the keeping of the Attorney General is the fortune of the French Canadians—their nationality.[124]

To overwhelm these opponents and to win approval of the Quebec Resolutions, Cartier used several tactics. One useful asset was the absence of the Rouges from the federation negotiations. Whereas Ontario was represented by both Brown and Macdonald, the Rouges were excluded from the coalition and the conferences in Charlottetown and Quebec City. French-Canadian Conservatives—Cartier, E. P. Taché, Hector Langevin, Jean-Charles Chapais, and Joseph Cauchon—spoke for French Canada. Only Cartier and Taché had more than regional stature; Taché was ninety years old, was absent from the Charlottetown

Conference, and died in 1866. Only four of the thirty-three delegates to the Quebec Conference were French Canadian. The conference negotiations were held *in camera* and no official minutes were kept.

Since the federation debate in Quebec took place in a "politics as usual" atmosphere, Cartier was able to exploit the vulnerability of the Rouges and his own image as *chef*. Moderate, respectable, and intelligent men favoured federation; its opponents, according to Cartier, were "extreme men," "socialists, democrats and annexationists."[125] *La Minerve* had another argument. Quebec faced "ruin" if it became obstructive: "When a general movement towards Confederation develops and when this movement is perfectly motivated, can we allow ourselves to stand in the way like an insuperable barrier, at the risk of bringing about their ruin and our own?"[126]

The Roman Catholic hierarchy's silence on the Confederation proposals allowed Cartier to claim clerical support. Since the conquest, the church in Quebec had supported established authority in the face of American invasions, the rebellions of 1837, and the annexation movement. During the Union period, conservative politicians—led by La Fontaine and Cartier—had cooperated with the Catholic hierarchy to impose social controls and to shape educational institutions and national societies.[127] Wealthy religious communities had supported government economic policy by sponsoring and investing in railways. Religious authorities had approved the judicial and landholding reforms accomplished in Quebec in the 1850s and 1860s, and federation, which created a conservative political structure with guarantees for Catholic rights, was a logical political extension.

Cartier publicly stated that Catholic clergy at all levels of the hierarchy supported federation because it protected their rights and limited political dissent: "I will say that the opinion of the clergy is favorable to Confederation. . . . In general, the clergy are the enemy of all political dissension and if they support this project, it is because they see in Confederation a solution to the difficulties which have existed for so long."[128] Although one of Bishop Bourget's spokesmen privately disputed Cartier's claim, his younger ultramontane colleague, Louis-François Laflèche, privately expressed strong support for Confederation.[129] Bourget himself was in Rome and quarrelling with Cartier and the Sulpicians over the division of the parish of Montreal. Other important Quebec clerics, particularly Bishops Baillargeon and Larocque, agreed that Confederation, if not desirable, was at least inevitable. *La Minerve* assured its readers that the Pope himself approved Confederation.[130]

In contrast to the ease with which he neutralized his Rouge critics, Cartier was extremely prudent with what John Rose described as "the undefined dread" towards Confederation shown by Quebec's English-speaking minority.[131] That community had long been favourably impressed by Cartier's conservatism, his pro-British views, his appointment to key civil service posts of anglophiles like P.J.O. Chauveau, his expansive economic policy, and his educational, civil code, and land-tenure reforms. As John Rose confidently expressed it, "We had the guarantee of the past to justify us in setting aside our fears. Whatever we desired our French-Canadian brethren at once gave us."[132]

Powerful Conservatives pushed hard for specific political, religious, and educational guarantees and Cartier acceded to demands concerning Protestant schools, the division of school taxes, and the granting of a fixed number of Eastern Township ridings. He further promised to use the federal government's veto in the case of a provincial act "hostile or destructive" to the English-speaking minority.[133] When a French-Canadian member received assurances in the assembly that the French language would be protected in the House of Commons, Cartier jumped up amidst cheers to promise that a similar provision would be made to protect English in the Quebec legislature.[134] These concessions and published statements that Cartier had given Galt a private, written pledge concerning English-speaking minority rights offended French-Canadian nationalists.[135] Even Conservative colleagues like Langevin protested against Cartier's compromises. In 1866 Cartier refused to name a French Canadian as chief justice of the Superior Court, telling Langevin that Galt and McGee agreed with him that "justice devra être rendue à l'élement britannique professionnel":

> A présent tout inéfficace qu'il soit, nous avons un juge en chef canadien français dans une cour, et il n'est que juste que le juge en chef de l'autre cour soit d'autre origine. Nous n'avons pas encore terminé toutes nos difficultés relatives à la Confédération et au gouvernement local pour le Bas Canada, et il ne serait pas sage d'exciter l'élément britannique du Bas Canada contre le gouvernement dans le moment.[136]

These efforts were appreciated: a month before Confederation, Galt publicly "rendered homage" to Cartier, noting the English-speaking community's "debt of gratitude" for the "elevated views" of Cartier and his colleagues.[137]

Since the government's majority in the united assembly easily approved the federation resolutions, Cartier did not have to call on direct support from the church and commercial élite until 1867. The federal elections of that year in Montreal-East demonstrated both the political potential of the city's working class and the élite's ability to channel and control dissatisfaction. Cartier was at the peak of his prestige, a minister of the crown, a lawyer for international concerns, and a recent house-guest of the Queen. His opponent, Médéric Lanctôt, was a young liberal-nationalist and local alderman.[138] A volatile lawyer and former partner of Wilfrid Laurier, Lanctôt had been associated with the Institut Canadien and a secret anti-Confederation society, le club Saint-Jean Baptiste (not to be confused with the St. Jean Baptiste Society). However, instead of forming an alliance of liberal moderates and campaigning aginst Confederation, Lanctôt made a direct appeal to working-class sentiment. His newspaper, *L'Union Nationale*, concentrated on basic issues like wages: "C'est parce que l'ouvrier, c'est parce que le peuple en général ne gagne pas assez; c'est parce que le travail manuel n'est pas assez rémunéré; c'est parce que le salaire de l'ouvrier agricole et industriel est insuffisant."[139]

In the spring of 1867 Lanctôt formed the Great Association of Workers. Incorporating European socialist principles, the association's program demanded Prudhomme-type councils to settle wage disputes, equality before the law, tariff protection for industry, and improved wages and working conditions.[140] It won support from twenty-five labour groups in Montreal and participated in two strikes. To force lower prices, Lanctôt opened food cooperatives. Three months before the election 15,000 workers and their families attended a workers' rally.

Faced with evident social unrest, the Montreal élite rallied quickly. The Conservative press made much of Cartier's triumphant visit to England and Rome. In his speeches Cartier defended Confederation although he never made it a central issue. Instead, he emphasized local issues, taking credit for the Victoria Bridge and noting the government's achievements in the construction of railroads, the abolition of seigneurial tenure, and the codification of Quebec civil law. The Grand Trunk Railway, the Allan Steamship Company, the Richelieu Navigation Company, the Montreal City Gas Company, the banks, and the manufacturers supported him; William Molson nominated him. Cartier had full control over government patronage in Quebec and had ample funds to distribute to the faithful.

Another substantial asset, despite his battle with Bishop Bourget, was support from important elements in the church. Even Bourget—while showing his displeasure with Cartier's newspaper by approving a new ultramontane paper, *Le Nouveau Monde*—issued two pastoral letters, May 23 and July 25, 1867, in which he urged voters to submit to authority and to respect the *status quo*.[141] Given his strength with the gallicans Cartier did not have to depend on Bourget's statements for evidence of clerical support. Other bishops, notably Larocque of St. Hyacinthe, publicized their support for the Conservatives. The clergy of St. Hyacinthe received Cartier with great ceremony during the election campaign; moreover, Cartier's managers used an election pamphlet, *Contre-poison*, to give wide distribution to Larocque's attack on radicalism.

Despite this support from the élite and the lukewarm help Lanctôt received from Liberals like Dorion, Cartier's winning margin was small. Although he won all three wards, the opposition's vote was impressive. Cartier defeated Lanctôt 2,433 to 2,085 and Ludger Labelle, his provincial opponent in the riding, 2,408 to 2,051. The opposition increased its share of the vote from 39 per cent in 1863 to 46 per cent in the 1867 federal election.[142]

Chapter Four
Institutions

From one political perspective, the Union period can be interpreted as three decades of political tinkering, ethnic elbowing, and the scratching for control of patronage. Alternatively, from a whig position the period represents the achievement of responsible government and Confederation. Considered from another standpoint, this evolution towards Canadian autonomy was only the highly visible political tip of even more significant change. The period, 1840–67, was one of fundamental social and economic change in which the La Fontaine-Cartier Conservatives—operating from a base of bourgeois values—succeeded in giving new form to the basic institutions of Quebec society. The abolition of seigneurial structures changed the nature of property ownership and exposed the entire social system to different forces. Quebec's system of commercial law—with its pre-French Revolution and pre-industrial revolution base—was adapted to nineteenth-century market, language, and labour realities by a revised civil code. With the failure of schemes such as the Royal Institutes to provide a rudder for Quebec education, the conservatives worked out a modus vivendi between church and state that ensured the revitalization of middle-class schools and the implementation of basic educational structures for the rural and urban proletariat. The latter constituency was isolated from reform and radical elements by the exploitation of both nationalism and the city's growing social service system by conservative fraternal, patriotic, and religious associations. Transportation policy represented another success for urban commercial values as evidenced by Quebec's imitation of other North American communities in undertaking an expansive and expensive program of railway construction.

By 1870 the unstable and ill-defined institutions of the rebellion period were barely recognizable. The province's revised legal machinery, economic structures, and conservative political apparatus, all had their anchors deep in the capitalist experience of western society; educational and benevolent institutions legitimized the image of a protected national and a static social hierarchy. In this changed order the Montreal bourgeoisie was in a position to neutralize opposition— whether it came from the rural parishes, from the factories, or from outside Quebec. Cartier, Conservative leader and lawyer for the largest railway and for the wealthiest element in the Roman Catholic Church, would symbolize this hegemony.

An early sign that Cartier understood the functions of social institutions was his role in shaping the St. Jean Baptiste Society. In the 1830s, St. Jean Baptiste banquets were raucous affairs in which the clergy had little influence. In 1843 the festival was revived, but instead of outdoor parties, songs, Chinese lanterns, champagne, and toasts to rebels and liberal clergymen, June 24 now had a special mass as its focal point. Headed by the British flag, the parade to Notre Dame church was given what the society's minutes described as "plus de solennité" by the participation of the St. Jacques Temperance Association.[1]

These celebrations were part of a larger effort in which clergy and bourgeoisie cooperated to fulfil the educational, health, fraternal, welfare, and nationalist needs of the Montreal populace, through the agency of temperance and colonization movements, reading-rooms, literary and scientific societies, various insurance and burial schemes, savings banks, schools, and hospitals. The St. Jean Baptiste Society was an early manifestation of this cooperation. Cartier was the first secretary of the society in 1843 and helped draft its original constitution. He sat on the executive committee, 1843 – 49, introduced its charter in the assembly, was elected vice president in 1850 and president in 1854.[2]

Before the formation of specialized aid-societies such as the St. Vincent de Paul Society in 1848 and the Union des Prières burial society in the 1850s, one of the St. Jean Baptiste Society's main tasks was to aid French-Canadian fire victims, the destitute, and the sick. Each unit of 100 members (a century) had a doctor who dispensed free medical care; the leader of each century reported members in distress to an Aid Committee. Society minutes give ample evidence of the clergy's active support for these activities. St. Jean Baptiste members participated in the Sulpicians' Fête Dieu, sent representatives to the laying of the St. Viateur church cornerstone, organized a reception for Bishop Bourget, and arranged a benefit for the Lower Canadian Colonization Society.

Cartier was particularly concerned to have all Catholic schoolchildren in the Montreal area attend the June 24 celebrations. He was also instrumental in giving the society a broader inter-ethnic base by bringing Wolfred Nelson and Lewis Drummond into the association.[3]

Education was another area of social organization characterized by immature institutional development. Efforts dating from 1801 to establish state-run common schools—the Royal Institutes of Learning—aborted, largely as a result of opposition from Catholic authorities. For their part, local curés, despite episcopal pressure, were largely apathetic in regard to the sponsorship of elementary schools in their parishes. Where schools did exist before 1840, the teachers, underpaid and on occasion illiterate, were largely drawn from the lay community. There were no teacher-training facilities and school inspections were often conducted by members of the assembly. Regional, ethnic, and religious rivalries and the fears of local school authorities for their autonomy impeded any educational initiatives by the government. School financing was characterized by frequent irregularities, the haphazard sale of Jesuit lands, and questionable bank loans. In 1836 there were twenty-five "phantom" or nonexistent schools receiving state subsidies.[4] As late as 1853 deputies and militia officers were still charged with distributing education funds; some simply pocketed monies made available for textbooks.[5]

General illiteracy was one result of these conditions. In the early 1840s only 12 per cent of rural francophones in Quebec could read and write.[6] Observers frequently related this illiteracy to outdated agricultural methods, low farm productivity, and a general indifference to "progress." Cartier's brother, for example, wrote from the Richelieu Valley that every county needed a special school to teach "scientific agriculture."[7] Other bourgeois leaders, concerned with mutinous popular elements, were aware of the important socializing function of a compulsory school system.

School construction in the 1840s by the Sulpicians and the vigorous recruitment of French teaching orders for the Montreal diocese by Bishop Bourget indicated escalating interest in education on the part of Catholic authorities. This coincided with a willingness on the part of the La Fontaine-Cartier Conservatives to accept a strong clerical influence in education.[8] Education bills after 1840 reflected this cooperation. In 1846 local priests or Protestant ministers were given the "exclusive" right to choose textbooks "having reference to religion or morals." Teacher-certification boards were established but members of religious orders were exempted from examination. Lay applicants for a teaching certificate needed a statement of moral character from their parish priest or minister.[9]

When Cartier assumed power in the mid-1850s systematic reform was unavoidable. The Rouges and Grits were increasingly vociferous in complaining about the clerical grip on education while Conservatives like Cartier were impressed by Egerton Ryerson's reforms in Ontario. In 1853 Cartier sat on the Sicotte committee of inquiry on the state of Quebec education. Its report was damning: the primary school system was inefficient, the public apathetic, the teachers incompetent, and half of the school commissioners illiterate. There was no standard curriculum or texts, school inspections were sporadic, government financing was disorganized, and teacher-training facilities almost nonexistent.[10] Various patchwork measures had failed. An attempt in 1851, for example, to establish a normal school had been blocked by competing regional and ethnic pressures. Nor could the well-organized Protestant lobby be ignored. Spokesmen like Galt and Christopher Dunkin demanded autonomy for Protestant schools, a larger share of school taxes, and compulsory bible study.[11] William Dawson, the aggressive new principal of McGill University, spent the 1855 Christmas recess in Toronto discussing university financing with Cartier; the Montreal *Gazette* championed higher teacher salaries so that Lower Canada could "overtake those who have gained a position in advance of them."[12]

Rural reaction to education measures was a further troubling factor. The act of 1846 imposed compulsory school taxes to be collected by government officials. While politicians and priests tried to legitimize the policy, many parishes over a period of years systematically refused to obey the law, to collect education taxes, or to return government reports. In 1849–50, violence broke out across Quebec. Children were kept out of school and reprisals occurred against local bourgeoisie or the curés. In Montreal a group of habitants marched on the governor's office. After the curé of Ile Bizard called for submission to the school law, his parishioners demonstrated in the church and threatened to burn down the presbytery. In several communities the barns of school commissioners were burned; in St. Michel d'Yamaska arsonists destroyed the schoolhouse.[13]

The government and clergy reacted with alacrity. Charges of arson and criminal conspiracy were laid and justices of the peace were sent to trouble spots. Prime Minister La Fontaine felt that these measures might not suffice and that unless the clergy gave more active support armed police or troops would have to be used: "l'on ne doit pas s'attendre qu'une police armée sera maintenue à grands frais ou que les troupes seront employées pour faire fonctionner cette loi."[14] In Quebec City Monseigneur Signay wrote to his clergy asking them to give their full support to school officials. Bishop Bourget took more dramatic action. Visiting Ile Bizard personally, he ordered the parish church locked until the law was obeyed.[15] Despite these measures there were still seven municipalities in 1855 not abiding by the act of 1846.

Cartier was an interested witness to these manifestations of rural opposition to taxation and compulsory education; his brother wrote complaining of the ignorance of Richelieu Valley farmers, his Sulpician friends were deeply involved financially in the construction of Christian Brothers' schools in working-class areas of Montreal, a bishop warned him that rebellion was imminent in the Bytown area if a means was not found to "calmer les esprits" on the schools issue.[16] As member of the assembly for a rural riding, president of the St. Jean Baptiste Society, and lawyer for a large industrial employer, he had a direct interest in social unrest, the education of the city's propertyless wage-earners, and the larger question of the adaptation of traditional French-Canadian values to an industrializing society. Since there was no minister of education, Cartier inherited the education dossiers when he became provincial secretary in 1855.

His most important subordinate was Pierre-Joseph-Olivier Chauveau, the new superintendent of education. Chauveau was easy-going, practical, politically adept, and had none of the Catholic puritanism of his predecessor, Jean-Baptiste Meilleur. An urbane lawyer and author, he had lived in the United States, spoke English well, and was amenable to the Protestant community. Cartier doubled the superintendent's salary and asked him to prepare legislation. The resulting thirty-five page report confirmed the Sicotte report's emphasis on the problems of teacher-training, sloppy school financing, and the excessive autonomy of local school boards. As well as weeding out illiterate teachers, Chauveau wanted a formal education budget and subsidies for books, maps, globes, and parish libraries.[17]

Less than a year after taking office Cartier introduced measures embodying Chauveau's proposals. Although he alluded to the rebellion against education taxes and the dangers of overtaxing municipalities, Cartier's legislation was clearly designed to accelerate the formation of a centralized, hierarchical, and integrated school system and included tough measures to force municipalities to return government reports and to collect school taxes. Model schools would be established in each municipality with subsidies from the central government; $4,000 was specifically budgeted to help educate the poor. The superintendent was given increased power to regulate both teachers and school boards.[18] Government grants to institutions of higher education would be financed from a reorganized investment fund based on revenues from the Jesuits' Estates.[19] Institutions applying for grants had to submit detailed reports concerning students, teachers, buildings, and texts. No book subsidies, for example, would be advanced without a full report from the institution on the state of their libraries.

Cartier's legislation regulated teachers, their training, their union, and their journal.[20] Teacher qualifications were upgraded and after 1856 female teachers who were not members of religious orders needed the same certification as males. To stimulate the supply of teachers, provision was made for three schools of education—an English-language normal school linked to McGill University, a French-language school to be located in Montreal, and a second French school attached to Laval University. Three schools, as compared with Ontario's single normal school, were necessary, Cartier explained, because of Quebec's religious and regional peculiarities.[21]

Chauveau played a prominent role in the formation of a teachers' association. The possibility that teachers might use it as a forum to criticize their employer was limited by the association's constitution which gave both the superintendent of common schools and the rector of the French-language normal school in Montreal the right to participate in meetings.[22] Another of Chauveau's enthusiasms, a periodical for teachers, was made possible by the Common School Act of 1856. Subsidized with an initial $1,800 government grant, *Le Journal de l'Instruction* had as its motto, *Rendre le peuple meilleur*. Its insignia had something for everyone—a cross implanted in a book which was in turn perched on a beaver, the whole surrounded by maple leaves.[23]

Given the alliance between Catholic clerics and conservative bourgeoisie, and the English-speaking minority's insistence on autonomy, it was clearly impossible to establish a Department of Education that would report to a secular minister of education. Instead an autonomous Council of Public Instruction was formed. This council supervised the administration of schools, regulated the examination, certification, and removal of teachers, and selected all texts except those dealing with religion and morals. The Cartier-Macdonald government named the first council in 1859. Eleven members were Roman Catholic,

VIOLENCE AND SOCIAL CONTROL: *above*, the burning of the Parliament Buildings, Montreal, 1849; *opposite above*, Grand Séminaire and Collège de Montréal, 1876, examples of the use of capital derived from the abolition of seigneurialism; *below*, logo, *Journal of Education*, 1857, a government-sponsored teachers' periodical that blended nationalism, religion, work, and science

four were Protestant; there were five clerics, eight lawyers, a doctor, and a notary.[24] The council immediately divided into Protestant and Catholic subcommittees to approve matters such as texts.

This granting of authority to a body relatively independent of government and the acceptance of a high degree of clerical participation in education permitted the La Fontaine-Cartier Conservatives to implement a centralized, compulsory, and comprehensive educational system—albeit divided into Catholic and Protestant sections. The result was a rapid growth in the number of schools and a subsequent rise in literacy before a levelling off after 1861.[25] The government was able to tighten control over all regions, imposing administrative order and forcing recalcitrant municipalities into line with new laws concerning taxes, school boards, and accounting procedures. While delegating important powers to religious authorities, the government's measures regulating normal schools, parish libraries, and model schools had clear implications for national ideology and social control.[26] Cartier's legislation forced local communities to tax themselves to pay the costs of primary education while using teachers, texts, and other norms approved by the central Council of Public Instruction.

The sharing of educational power with Protestant and Catholic authorities coincided with similar cooperation in the institutionalization process in the political, economic, and welfare sectors. Before establishing a new parish—partly a civic responsibility—Cartier carefully corresponded with the local bishop who replied with specific suggestions concerning acceptable officials.[27] During the passage of his 1856 education bills Cartier rebuffed Dorion's attempts to finance primary education with revenues from the Jesuits' Estates and his party voted down a Rouge amendment proposing mixed schools in which all religious instruction would be banned. In his first year as provincial secretary, conservatives attacked his school-audit bill, predicting that Catholic institutions would reject government aid "with contempt."[28] In fact, the Catholic hierarchy publicly supported Cartier's measures. The first Council of Public Instruction included three Catholic clerics—the bishop of St. Hyacinthe, the rector of Laval University, and the Irish curé of St. Patrick's Church.[29] Although the church had opposed earlier teacher-training legislation, Bishop Baillargeon appeared at the opening of the Laval Normal School and noted that "the only thing we fear is education without religion and without morality . . . . As this Normal School had been established on the well-avowed principle that religion must be the basis of education we, for our part, are glad to cooperate in the great work."[30]

Wooing Protestant support in the education sector took time. In 1856 Galt voiced fears about the powers granted to a French-speaking and Catholic superintendent of schools. Jasper H. Nicolls, the principal of Bishop's College, responded to the government's new administrative procedures by submitting only "unofficial" reports. "The Superintendent may be right," he observed, "in asking for information about Colleges such as some of the Roman Catholic or 'Lower Canada Colleges' in Montreal, but certainly he cannot expect this College to put itself under him."[31] Over the next decade Cartier and Chauveau placated these fears by budgetary favours and by emphasizing Protestant autonomy. Instead of dividing the budget of the three normal schools according to population, they granted one-third of the budget to the McGill Normal School.[32] The division of the Council of Public Instruction into separate Catholic and Protestant subcommittees was reassuring as was the government's encouragement of the publication of an English edition of the *Journal de l'Instruction* with different contents. Nor was the government aggressive on the language issue. Presenting the normal school bill, Cartier promised that English would be the sole language of instruction at the McGill Normal School.[33]

Reform of Quebec's legal institutions was another important element in the formation of a modern, centralized commercial state. During the French régime the common law of northern France—*la coutume de Paris*—had been applied to Canada. After the conquest the British government applied English criminal law but retained French civil law in Lower Canada. Lord Durham had been baffled by the resulting legal system, "a patchwork," "a mass of incoherent and conflicting laws, part French, part English, and with the line between each very confusedly drawn."[34] Reflecting its largely feudal origins, the Custom of Paris integrated property rights into a seigneurial, family, and religious framework; since property rights were often not absolute, land was in many cases inalienable. A legal structure based on these principles was incompatible with the changing capitalism of nineteenth-century Quebec. By the 1850s the situation had become even more complicated since in English-speaking areas, such as the Eastern Townships, English civil law was sometimes used.

Codification was also essential from a technical point of view. Since Canada's separation from France predated the Napoleonic Code, French civil law used in Lower Canada was a badly organized mixture of Roman, Germanic, and French traditions. In their demands for an organized, uniform, and "progressive" body of commercial law,

bourgeois leaders employed the same rhetoric that was used to abolish
the seigneurial system, to institute educational reforms, and to justify
heavy public subsidies for transportation projects: codification, according to one lawyer, would "increase and facilitate business relations,"
would ensure "stability," and act as a "conservatory barrier."[35]

The civil code governed property relationships and like the abolition
of the seigneurial system was at the very core of the institutional
reorganization of Quebec. Cartier, attorney general and senior partner
in a commercial law firm, was well aware of the code's significance,
describing it as "the most pregnant source of national greatness"; if
"the inhabitants of Lower Canada wished that their country should
increase in strength and power, nothing was better calculated to promote and perpetuate it than a revised civil code."[36]

Always sensitive to the views of the English-speaking community,
Cartier pointed out that British criminal law—"the best in the
world"—would not be affected and that codification would serve "not
only the interests of my people, but also those of the other inhabitants of
Lower Canada, English, Scots and Irish."[37] He felt that many com-
plaints originated in the lack of an English translation of the code. "The
great body of laws [in Lower Canada] exist," according to Cartier's bill,
"only in a language which is not the mother tongue of the inhabitants
. . . of British origin." The revised code was to be drawn up "in the
French and English languages, and the two texts, when printed, shall
stand side by side."[38] One of the three commissioners was to be anglophone and their two secretaries—one French-speaking, the other
English-speaking—were to be fluently bilingual.

Cartier stage-managed the whole process of codification over an
eight-year period. He presented the reform bill, formed the commission,
named its members, chaired the legislative committee which examined
the commission report, and used the government's majority to achieve
passage of the revised code through the assembly.

Opening civil law to the process of codification had its hazards.
George Brown immediately proposed a wider legal reform leading to
the unification of Canadian law. Cartier rejected this. The old French
code was to be simplified and translated into English but Quebec's
distinct legal system had to be maintained. Nor would he accede to
opposition attempts to have the commission named by the assembly
instead of the government. Cartier appointed safe, Conservative vete-
rans who had moved from politics to the bench. When La Fontaine
declined to chair the commission, René-Edouard Caron and A.-N.

Morin, both Quebec city judges, and Charles Dewey Day, a Superior Court judge in Montreal, were named. The commission rented premises in Quebec City, in a building owned by Caron, and held their first meeting in October 1859.[39] Between 1861 and 1864 they submitted eight reports which were referred to a special legislative committee chaired by Cartier. This committee met nineteen times in the winter of 1865 and then submitted the code for approval by the assembly.[40] One year before Confederation the new code went into effect.

Concurrently with codification, Cartier presented two bills that aided the development of a uniform, structured legal system. The first bill reorganized the Lower Canadian court system, established nineteen judicial districts, and provided £75,000 for court houses and jails. The new districts made Circuit Courts superfluous. Circuit Court judges were merged into an enlarged Superior Court of nineteen judges; four Superior Court judges were stationed in Montreal, three in Quebec City, and the rest in smaller centres.[41] The second act clarified application of the revised civil code to the Eastern Townships.[42]

Like the civil code, the Lower Canadian landholding system was perceived as a barrier to the development of a stable, centralized state and to the implementation of new social, commercial, agricultural, and transportation measures. A legacy from New France, seigneurial tenure set the economic and social tone of rural French Canada and was still a force in mid-nineteenth-century Montreal.[43]

Despite the weakness of the seigneurial class, and the system's inability to cope with either the agricultural or demographic crisis, seigneurialism was a tenacious institution synonymous with traditional rural life, the family economy, a paternalistic, feudal church, and relative independence from state legal and political power. By regulating economic relationships as part of a social whole instead of in individualistic terms it had offered a structured defence against both the encroachment of the central government and the integration of rural Quebec into an urban market economy. The Lake of Two Mountains seigneury, to take a large example, had 1,260 *censitaires*. Each of these seigneurial tenants had obligations that included annual rents, church tithes, milling, fishing and ferry fees, sales taxes, and death duties; the seigneur, for his part, had diverse obligations concerning mill facilities, justice, woodcutting, and road maintenance; the local clergy had educational, religious, and welfare responsibilities. This complicated, hierarchical, and interdependent system of property, work, and social institutions impeded land speculation, transportation development, the settlement of immigrants, and the implementation of a changed social or work ethic. The use of common nineteenth-century commercial devices such as the mortgage was rendered difficult by the absence of outright individual title and the priority of seigneurs over other creditors.[44]

Traditionally marginal to the feudal structure, the bourgeoisie had goals antithetical to seigneurialism. For security, law, and business organization, merchants, lawyers, entrepreneurs, and bureaucrats looked to the central government; urban-oriented, they operated in a capitalist framework that emphasized individual rights, credit, and labour as a purchasable commodity. Although they themselves owned a significant number of seigneuries, the English-speaking commercial community had long singled out seigneurialism as an anachronism that, according to the chairman of the assembly's abolition committee, was "opposed to the progressive spirit."[45] Another land and railroad developer, Alexander Galt, described the seigneurial system as "repressive of the industry of the people, degrading them in character and effectively precluding Lower Canada from sharing in the flow of population and wealth."[46]

Given the ethnic component of the crisis of the period 1800–38, and the patriotes' division over social goals, the attitude of the francophone bourgeoisie to seigneurial tenure was more complicated. Radicals lumped seigneurialism with Catholicism, the monarchy, and other institutions deemed reactionary; important leaders like Papineau, however, defended the seigneurial system as a bulwark of French-Canadian values. This ambivalence disappeared in the 1840s as bourgeois opponents of abolition like Denis-Benjamin Viger were overwhelmed by the La Fontaine group.[47]

Cartier's merchant-family background, his profession, his urban business interests, and his railway clients made him a stereotype opponent of seigneurialism and an important agent in legitimizing the landholding revolution among the rural populace and particularly in negotiating the special case of abolition on the island of Montreal. As with his other institutional reforms, he based his argument for freehold tenure on the need to facilitate economic development and social control.

Convinced of the positive economic and social function of individual property ownership, Cartier felt that the major "vice" of seigneurial tenure was that it "entrave l'esprit d'entreprise."[48] This repression of individual initiative, he explained, had repercussions on markets, expansion, and mobility; Upper Canada, for instance, had 200 flour mills while Lower Canada produced inferior flour and had only two mills producing for export.[49] Cartier also appreciated the important capital accumulation that would accompany commutation and expressed regret that seigneurs could not be immediately reimbursed so that they could make lump investments.[50]

Cartier introduced the problem of rural instability into the seigneurial debate. Hostility to government education measures, emigration, and a large floating population of landless day labourers disturbed authorities. In some areas up to 40 per cent of family heads were unable to obtain land but remained in their home parishes as a "proletariat de jeunes."[51] Cartier suggested that an old-world, outdated landholding system like seigneurial tenure could lead to riots and even "socialist doctrines"; the cause of order would be helped by abolishing it.[52]

For thirty years the seigneurial question was debated in the press and before various legislative committees. Between 1841 and 1851 nineteen resolutions and 81 petitions calling for the modification or abolition of seigneurial tenure were presented to the assembly.[53] Finally, in 1851 Lewis Drummond chaired a committee which hammered out an abolition bill and over the next three years found compromises for the delicate issues of compulsory commutation and reimbursement for absentee seigneurs and third-party owners. Passed by the assembly in 1853, the bill stalled in the Legislative Council.

Faced with scepticism on the part of the habitants and strong opposition from many seigneurs, government spokesmen such as J.-C. Taché asked their rural audiences to look at abolition "in a broader light." The seigneurial system obstructed railway construction and hurt "society at large." "In a case like this," Taché declared, "and in that of the foundation or enlargement of Towns, or the establishment of mills or factories, it is not the Censitaire, the present occupier of rural property, who suffers the greatest wrong, but the mechanic, the capitalist, and as a consequence, society in general, whose progress may be retarded and even paralyzed."[54] Montreal-area politicians organized abolition meetings to rally rural opinion. Verchères was typical. Cartier appeared at local meetings, outlined why he had voted twice in favour of abolition, denied that the costs of the seigneurial commission were extravagant, carefully explained the bill's financial details for *censitaires*, and concluded that abolition was in the interest of the habitants. His riding passed an abolition resolution which attacked the Legislative Council's

delaying tactics as "unjust and cavalier." English-speaking businessmen were particularly pleased with the efforts of their francophone
peers. Francis Hincks felt that this Montreal-led agitation and the
resulting change in rural opinion were crucial in forcing passage of the
bill in November 1854.[55]

Cartier's most important function in the abolition of seigneurial tenure
was resolving the special problems of the island of Montreal, a seigneury in the possession of the Sulpicians, a Roman Catholic religious
order. Any adjustment in seigneurial dues—the Sulpicians' major
source of income—had repercussions for the whole community since
the order named parish priests for the entire island of Montreal, was
a central component in the alliance between the La Fontaine-Cartier
conservatives and gallican Catholics, and acted as a pivotal force in the
city's educational and welfare institutions. Seigneurialism on Sulpician
lands was partly abolished in 1840, exempted from the general Lower
Canadian legislation of 1854, and finally officially abolished by bills
presented by Cartier in 1859—60.

La Compagnie de Saint-Sulpice—the Sulpicians— was founded in
Paris in the 1640s in response to the Council of Trent's call for new
seminaries to train parish priests. The Sulpicians were early characterized by their union of parish and seminary: the founder of the order
was at the same time superior of the seminary and curé of the local
parish of Saint-Sulpice—a practice which would be repeated in
Montreal. Although they worked closely with French bishops in the
selection and education of priests, the Sulpicians always claimed independence from episcopal jurisdiction.[56] Again there was a parallel with
Montreal where—over 150 years before the establishment of the diocese of Montreal—the Sulpicians founded a largely autonomous domain. A wealthy community recruiting their members from the sons of
officers, judges, surgeons, and small landowners, the Sulpicians became
the foremost seminarians in France after the Jesuits were expelled in
1762. Opposed to ultramontanism, they tempered their Catholicism
with a strong measure of gallicanism; this flexibility to the exigencies of
civil power helped the company survive the French Revolution.

The Sulpician presence in Canada dates from the origins of Montreal
in the 1640s and the foundation of its seigneurial, benevolent, educational, and religious institutions. They participated in la Société Notre
Dame de Montréal, an association established to provide religious and
social services to natives and colonists, and in 1663 acquired the seigneury of Montreal from its bankrupt owners. To fulfil their expanding

responsibilities the Sulpicians established the Seminary of Montreal and later added large seigneuries at Two Mountains and St. Sulpice (see figure 1).[57]

In addition to their religious duties, the Sulpicians in New France had various civic functions, serving as soldiers, teachers, record-keepers, seigneurs, and colonization agents.[58] Sulpicians organized the parish structure on the island of Montreal, including Montreal's own parish, Notre Dame. They worked with the Indians first on the outskirts of Montreal and later at their Lake of Two Mountains seigneury; the first significant fortifications in Montreal were built at the personal expense of a Sulpician priest; Sulpicians directed settlement throughout the island of Montreal, sponsored the immigration of 100 colonist families, and kept official community records. The Seminary of Montreal retained its founder's suspicion of diocesan control. Successive superiors carefully united seigneurial, seminarian, and parish privileges so as to emphasize their independence from the bishop of Quebec. They also copied the mother house's gallicanism and shared power with civil authorities; aside from their religious duties, their responsibilities included middle-class education, welfare, supervision of female religious communities, mission services, and the management of three large seigneuries.

The cession of New France to Britain in 1763 placed the seminary in an official limbo that lasted until the British government confirmed its rights in 1840. In 1764 the company declined Britain's offer to liquidate their Canadian holdings and to return to France. Instead the mother house in Paris transferred ownership of the Seminary of Montreal to the twenty-eight Sulpicians who agreed to remain in Canada.[59] On condition that no new French Sulpicians be admitted and that the Canadian house remain completely independent from Paris, British officials allowed the seminary to retain its property. Faced with slow strangulation the seminary's position deteriorated and by 1790 only ten aged Sulpicians remained in Canada.[60] This decline was reversed by the French Revolution and the subsequent arrival of eleven emigré Sulpicians. Within ten years the seminary had recovered materially and was constructing a new school with seigneurial profits from the high wheat prices of the Napoleonic wars.

This prosperity did not mask the seminary's delicate official position. Sulpician allegiance to the Pope was awkward in an empire in which it was illegal to acknowledge the authority of a foreign power.[61] A major landowning institution, the seminary did not have a British charter and therefore lacked corporate status to enforce property rights. For decades, powerful members of the English-speaking business community accused the seminary of blocking commercial development by its seigneurial privileges in urban Montreal, while many French-Canadian bourgeois, influenced by European secularism and American liberalism, challenged the Sulpicians' seigneurial, educational, and social privileges.

Harassed and insecure, the Sulpicians received a windfall with the rebellions of 1837–38 which gave them an opportunity to demonstrate their loyalty to British civil power. They urged enlistment in the government militia and helped defuse Irish unrest in Montreal; the superior met with Papineau and his wife and encouraged them to leave the city, and burned two letters he received demanding that the seminary's wealth be used to support the *patriotes*. After the collapse of the rebellions, he acted as a mediator, discussed the exile problem with the governor, and carried safe-conduct passes to rebels in the United States.[62]

Reward, for what one British peer described as "having prevented the outbreak of sedition and violence in the city of Montreal," came with the granting of a new charter to the Sulpicians. In 1838 Charles Buller, Durham's secretary, met with the Sulpician superior and worked out an accord. Two years later the seminary, which had received its original letters-patent from Louis XIV, was reincorporated by the Ordinance of 1840. The seminary was granted freedom of recruitment, its social and educational responsibilities were defined, and its property rights confirmed; as a recognized religious corporation it could now protect its interests with the force of law. The ordinance was, as the Duke of Wellington remarked, a "total departure . . . from the principle of the Reformation."[63]

With this new legitimacy the Sulpicians expanded enthusiastically, using income derived from seigneurial dues, commutations, sale of produce from their own farms, land sales, and rents from urban properties. They tripled their membership between 1840 and 1875, and made substantial investments in organs, religious works of art, furniture, and furnaces. In 1844 they opened l'Oeuvre des bons livres which became the city's major reading room. They built the Grand Séminaire and in 1865 covered their games court.[64]

The crown's recognition of Sulpician rights coincided with La Fontaine's growing political importance and the rapprochement of his social group with the gallican clergy. Baptized, confirmed, married, and buried by the Sulpicians, renting their office and store space, reading in their library and listening to their sermons, the conservative bourgeoisie accepted strong clerical participation in educational and social matters. Their newspaper organs took proclerical positions. *La Minerve* lauded Sulpician heroism in the Irish immigration sheds and gave full obituaries to subsequent Sulpician cholera victims.[65] The alliance was also evident in education legislation and in the bourgeoisie's presence in church-sponsored colonization, temperance, and benevolent societies. This cooperation was reinforced by an old-boy network of school, business, social, and political ties. Cartier was educated in the Sulpicians' Collège de Montréal and three of his classmates became priests; he acted as the order's lawyer, and named the superior as an executor of his estate. His state funeral was held in their church; he is buried in the parish cemetery.

For their part, the Sulpicians became more tolerant of French Canada, its nationalism, and its liberal professions; they supported Conservative candidates in election campaigns, cooperated in imposing social order, and for the first time actively recruited French-Canadian members to their order. A major consumer, landowner, and source of capital, the seminary cemented ties with its lay allies by buying their goods and employing their legal, architectural, notarial, banking, and medical services. In 1841 La Fontaine and his law partner and brother-in-law, Joseph-Amable Berthelot, began receiving Sulpician legal work. When La Fontaine moved to the bench, Cartier and Berthelot—school friends from the Collège de Montréal—formed a partnership. Their firm directed political lobbying for the Sulpicians, handled some of their investments, and prepared the legal ammunition for the seminary's long battle with Bishop Bourget. The seminary was a major investor in the stock of another Cartier client, the Grand Trunk Railway. For its part, the Grand Trunk was an important buyer of Sulpician lands.[66]

To Cartier, the seminary was a public utility with social and educational functions that were essential to Montreal's prosperity.[67] Provision of schools for the rapidly growing urban proletariat was an urgent priority. Since their own schools catered to the élite, the seminary turned to the Christian Brothers, a French order which specialized in popular education and which had a tradition of cooperation with the Sulpicians. Negotiations began in 1829 and eight years later the Christian Brothers accepted the Sulpician terms. The first brothers were welcomed at the Seminary of Montreal in the midst of the rebellions of 1837; by 1882 there were 294 Christian Brothers in Canada teaching over 10,000 pupils.[68] The Sulpicians subsidized convent schools and orphanages, constructed schools in working-class neighbourhoods, paid for lay teachers, caretakers, firewood, school taxes, and insurance, and helped the Christian Brothers implement commercial and industrial training at Lasalle College.

Turbulence in Montreal's expanding Irish community was a recurring threat to authority. The Sulpicians made cash contributions to the Irish poor, recruited Irish priests and paid for their training in France, sponsored their schools, subsidized St. Patrick's Church, and made an annual contribution to their hospital.[69] Nor did they neglect their rural parishioners. The Christian Brothers received help in establishing an agricultural school on the seminary's seigneury at Two Mountains in 1851 and in the same year a Sulpician priest organized a burial society for the poor, the Union des Prières.[70]

This alliance between the conservative bourgeoisie and the Sulpicians was marred by the continued existence of seigneurial tenure on the seminary's lands. The Ordinance of 1840 permitted the transformation of seigneurial tenure into freehold ownership but the process was voluntary and could only be initiated by the tenant (*censitaire*). Many urban proprietors took advantage of this option; by the late 1850s the seminary had received over £100,000 in commutations from the city and parish of Montreal. However, the seminary's habitants—fearful that a change in tenure would lead to loss of their land and inhibited by the costs—showed little enthusiasm for converting their properties to freehold tenure. By March 1852 only twelve of the Sulpicians' 1,260 *censitaires* at the Two Mountains seigneury and ten habitants at the seigneury of St. Sulpice had commuted their properties; in parishes on the island of Montreal, but outside the city, one-third of the habitants had commuted by 1859.[71]

Despite the satisfaction of their Sulpician allies with the status quo, the Montreal bourgeoisie could not permit seigneurialism in the Montreal area to remain indefinitely as an anachronism in relation to the freehold system prevailing elsewhere in North America. Voluntary, snail's-pace abolition was obstructive of administrative and judicial reform, transportation development, and the implementation of an ethic based on individualism. Cartier wanted seigneurial abolition to progress apace with his civil code reforms and worried that at the prevailing rate of commutations, seigneurialism in rural districts around Montreal would last another 200 years.[72] He was also concerned by what he called the seminary's tax "sur l'industrie et l'activité des habitants." When land on the seminary's seigneuries—and this included urban property in Montreal—changed hands, approximately 8 per cent of the sale price was owed to the seminary as a change-of-ownership tax (*lods et ventes*). As a result, any vendor who had improved his property (i.e. constructed a building) lost 8 per cent of his investment.[73]

Attempts to include Sulpician lands in the general seigneurial abolition bill of 1854 incited a sharp reaction. Joseph Comte, the seminary's influential business manager, wrote four letters to Cartier and a fifth to Lewis Drummond demanding "une exception totale" from the proposed bill. He reminded Cartier of the seminary's role "au bien de la religion, à l'éducation gratuite des pauvres, au soutien des invalides, des orphelins et en aumônes aux malheureux de toutes conditions." The Sulpician Indian mission at Lake of Two Mountains acted as a force for social order; its "destruction" would lead to starvation and force the Indians to "redevenir barbares." Asking for special treatment in "le nom de la Religion" and in "l'intérêt du pays," Comte insisted that the Ordinance of 1840 was a "treaty" and therefore could not be changed without the approval of both parties. In the face of this pressure, the complicated arrangements of 1840, and the special social functions of the Sulpicians, the government exempted the Seminary of Montreal from the Seigneurial Act of 1854.[74]

In 1858–59 Cartier, now attorney general and anxious to dispose of the issue, again consulted the Sulpicians. He told them it was increasingly difficult to "stifle demands" for the application of the 1854 legislation to the Montreal area and warned of "disagreeable agitation" if abolition was not forthcoming. The seminary insisted that important concessions be granted if compulsory commutation was applied to their seigneuries: they asked for the inclusion of overdue seigneurial dues in commutation settlements, a second twenty-year delay in the sale of their 270-acre St. Gabriel farm on the western limits of the city, broader rights to invest the capital which compulsory commutations would bring into their coffers, and freedom to subdivide and sell their own lots at market prices. Each of these conditions appeared in the bill presented by Cartier.[75]

In March 1859 Cartier negotiated the financial clauses of his abolition bill with seminary officials. Together they worked out the price of wheat to be used in commutations, the amount of the crown's lump settlement, and the disposition of feudal dues on government buildings in Montreal. In the final stages he invited the superior to Toronto. The superior was pleased that Cartier had settled the matter privately, "sans intervention des commissaires, sans cadastre et sans aucune recherche ultérieure."[76] Before presentation of the bill in the Legislative Assembly the terms were sent back to Montreal for approval by the seminary's governing council.[77]

Cartier was able to defuse the parliamentary opposition by including equalization payments in his bill. Upper Canada and the Eastern Townships were given indemnities proportional to amounts paid to Lower Canadian seigneurs. Replying to charges of favouritism to his clerical allies, he insisted that the seminary would have received £30,000 more if it had been included in the bill of 1854. Finally, he emphasized the Sulpicians' important social role in Montreal and the free education they provided for 5,000 children.[78] These tactics split the opposition. Dorion and most Rouges supported Cartier's bill and held a special caucus to protest the Grits' violent ethnic, sectional, and religious attacks on French-Canadian institutions. Despite a 39-hour Grit filibuster, the bill passed easily.[79]

The acts of 1859–69 brought the form of property ownership in the Montreal area into line with the administrative, judicial, and political reforms applied in Quebec in the Union period. Urban expansion was facilitated by the subdivision and sale of the St. Gabriel farm and religious fiefs within the city, and land and labour were opened to free exchange. [80] The abolition of seigneurial tenure was a "social revolution," Alexander Galt told a London audience, "effected at a most trivial cost."[81]

For their part, the Sulpicians—consulted at every stage of the legislation—adapted effectively. In 1840 they were the symbol of seigneurialism in Montreal; thirty years later they were an important accessory to the process of urbanization and industrialization, charged with financing and supervising many of the city's most important social institutions. Although its source changed from feudal dues to returns on capital investment, Sulpician income remained more than adequate to discharge these responsibilities. Their income from commutations rose from $18,275 in 1865 to $31,996 in 1871. Their portfolio in 1865 included stock in the Grand Trunk Railway and bonds of the City of Montreal and the Port of Montreal; in 1871 they used Cartier's office to invest in the North Shore Railway and in the same year they began investing in mortgages.[82]

Cartier's efforts on behalf of the Seminary of Montreal were only part of his relationship with religious authorities in the Montreal area. He was an early supporter of colonization, promoted temperance in his first political campaign, and was a perennial activist in the St. Jean Baptiste Society. Ceremony was important to both priests and politicians and Cartier was highly visible at clerical funerals, convent graduations, and the ordination of bishops. Papal independence from Italian nationalists was of concern to Catholics in the 1850s and 1860s:

Cartier spoke out strongly in favour of the Pope's temporal powers and made a well-publicized contribution of $200 for the defence of papal territories.[83]

Local priests acted as intermediaries for their communities and lobbied with bureaucrats and businessmen. Clergymen wrote to Cartier concerning mail service, patronage appointments, or the choice of political candidates.[84] The higher clergy was always watchful for legislation with implications for morals, the family, education, or Catholic religious practice. Cartier's position was complicated because of the necessity for national leaders to compromise with non-Catholic sectors of the Canadian populace. Secular schools, marriage, and divorce were particularly delicate matters. In 1859 *La Minerve* strongly attacked a petition for permission to remarry from an Upper Canadian Protestant and in the same year Cartier voted against a bill that, in certain cases, would permit divorce among Protestants.[85] During the civil code reforms, the Confederation debate in Quebec, and again in 1872, Cartier discussed marriage law with the Quebec bishops.[86]

More difficult to avoid was entanglement in the Seminary of Montreal's long struggle with the bishop of Montreal. With its ingredients of gallicanism and ultramontanism, a French versus a French-Canadian institution, and a rich, landed order against an ambitious prelate, the struggle cut deep in Montreal, was a permanent feature of Cartier's public life, and an important factor in his political defeat in 1872.

The struggle between the seminary and the bishop dated from the 1820s. Permanent curés of the parish of Montreal, the Sulpicians objected to the infringement of their powers implicit in the establishment of a diocese in Montreal. They opposed construction of St. Jacques Church, a non-Sulpician church, and were not placated by the nomination in 1836 of a Sulpician, Jean-Jacques Lartigue, as the first bishop of Montreal. The situation was aggravated by the nomination of Ignace Bourget as bishop of Montreal in 1840. He did not have a Sulpician training or outlook and, as Lartigue's secretary and vicar-general, had felt snubbed by the Sulpicians for two decades. Whereas the Sulpicians bent with temporal realities, Bourget battled against Montreal's secularism, was uncompromising with civil authority, and suspicious of bourgeois leaders like Cartier.[87] Irascible, overworked, and often ill, he was critical of the Sulpicians' choice of school textbooks, of their laxness in applying strict Roman ritual, and of their links to Jansenism which had brought France "les horribles malheurs de la grande révolution."[88]

In 1831 a first appeal was made to Rome to settle the problem of jurisdiction in the parish of Montreal. Unresolved, the conflict festered. Bourget insisted that, although the Sulpician superior had the right of nomination, the parish priest of Montreal was "entirely dependent upon the bishop."[89] The Sulpicians expressed willingness to build new parish churches but guarded their power over financing and the nomination of priests. After the fire of 1852 the seminary dragged its feet in the choice of a new site and in the financing of a new cathedral. For his part, Bourget succeeded in blocking the reelection of Joseph-Vincent Quiblier as Sulpician superior in 1846. When Cartier assumed major political office in the mid-1850s hostilities had spread to other sectors with important political and social implications: Jesuit education in Montreal, establishment of a Catholic university in Montreal, supervision of the city's Irish, and the issuing of registers to new parishes.

As debate over the division of the parish of Montreal escalated into the press and Legislative Assembly and finally back to Rome, Cartier's sympathies were never in doubt. His law firm defended the Sulpicians in the civil courts and he himself later pleaded in Rome on their behalf. Rome's decree in 1865 in favour of Bourget did not settle the question. In long, detailed memoranda written on behalf of the seminary, Cartier argued that Bourget was acting "contrary to the law" in registering births and deaths other than in the official register in the Sulpicians' Notre Dame Church. In addition, until the provincial government conferred civil authority on other parishes, all marriages in Montreal had to be performed at Notre Dame. Cartier's influence with the Chauveau administration ensured obstruction in the granting of this status to new parishes created by the bishop.[90] As the election of 1872 was to demonstrate, the cresting of ultramontanism on the issues of papal zouavism, the New Brunswick schools question, and the programme catholique would sweep away Cartier as an early victim.

Cartier's power in Montreal depended on his solid base in important institutions, as lawyer for the city's richest religious order, as an officer in the law society, benevolent associations, militia, and harbour board, as a director of several banking, insurance, and transportation companies, as a member through marriage of a prominent bourgeois family, as chef of the Conservative party, and as patron of the local government bureaucracy. Along with the Seminary of Montreal, the Grand Trunk Railway was Cartier's most important source of strength. Like the seminary it was an international organization for which Cartier—the most important Quebec Conservative, cabinet member, and chairman

The transportation revolution: Victoria Bridge, Grand Trunk Railway

Grand Trunk train near Chaudière, Que.

of the assembly's railway committee—served as the local legal and political agent. The most active period of his career coincided with the expansion in Montreal of the Grand Trunk and the seminary, his later years with the Pacific Railway's challenge to the Grand Trunk and a renewed ultramontane offensive against both his clerical allies and his own social group.

Chartered in 1854 and completed in 1860, the Grand Trunk extended from Sarnia, Ontario, through Montreal and the Eastern Townships to Portland, Maine. With its technical and capital demands and its dependence on Atlantic steamshipping and foreign markets, the railway quickly outgrew the resources of its local promoters. The railway's major bankers, lawyers, brokers, and contractors were British. The London board of directors, named in part by the Canadian government and chaired by Thomas Baring, made the key financial decisions and leaned heavily on the local directors, many of whom were cabinet ministers in the Canadian government.[91] The extent of head-office control increased as the company's financial position deteriorated. Canadian officers travelled to England and returned with escalating demands for public subsidies. In 1856 Sir William Napier was sent out with what the Canadian board's minutes called "Baring's instructions." Two years later the vice-president rented a house in Toronto during the legislative session so that he could watch proceedings. By 1860 the Glyn and Baring houses' liability on their Grand Trunk holdings had risen to over £600,000.[92] Management of the company was tightened and C.J. Brydges, the tough general manager, was ordered to return weekly reports directly to London. Long, detailed letters sent to Cartier by Baring and Brydges make it clear that effective power in the company had passed to London officials and their on-site professional manager.[93]

The Grand Trunk pioneered in the special relationship which railways have had with the state in Canada: the Grand Trunk and government were mutually supportive institutions, often scrapping but sharing fundamental objectives.[94] The Grand Trunk carried the staples, the mail, the militia, and the politicians; in 1854 its payroll was £15,000 a day.[95] Its influence on freight rates, routes, labour markets, elections, and industrial growth assured the railway of a position at the core of Canadian political life. It financed campaigns, employed important politicians, rewarded regions, and distributed sinecures, cash, or free passes; important political friends drank company champagne and travelled on special trains.[96] The state promoted, gave respectability to, and subsidized the railway with a thicket of guarantees, monopolies, loans, land grants, and cash subsidies. Blatantly interventionist in sheltering the Grand Trunk, the government blocked competing railways, established flexible laws, and chartered construction firms, banks, or insurance companies needed by the railway. Politicians like John A. Macdonald and Cartier were proud of their service to the railway. "I have as you know," Macdonald explained in 1882, "uniformly backed the GTR since 1854 and won't change my course now."[97] Cartier repeated several times that introduction of the Grand Trunk charter was the proudest moment of his life: "I am prouder of that than any other action of my life. Even today it is the Grand Trunk which is the principal cause of public prosperity."[98]

Years before taking a seat in the assembly Cartier was active in stimulating public support for railways and in encouraging municipal subsidies for railways that were ultimately incorporated into the Grand Trunk. In 1846 construction began on both the St. Lawrence and Atlantic Railway and its American counterpart, the Atlantic and St. Lawrence, two railways that, when linked, would join Montreal and Portland, Maine, an ice-free Atlantic port 100 miles closer to Montreal than Boston. Appearing at an 1846 railway rally chaired by La Fontaine, Cartier spoke after Francis Hincks and Lewis Drummond. Without railways, he told the crowd, it was "impossible" for a country to enjoy prosperity.[99] With vigorous expansion of railways, he speculated, Montreal might become the entrepôt between Europe and America, East and West.

By 1849 the British railway boom had collapsed, private investment had evaporated, and the St. Lawrence and Atlantic was stalled in the Quebec countryside with only forty miles of track laid. Since seventy-five miles of completed track were necessary for government assistance under the recently passed Guarantee Act, the developers turned to municipal subsidies and local leaders like Cartier. Far from having any ethnic, religious, or pastoral bias against railways, Cartier—son-in-law of the mayor, protegé of the prime minister, and ambitious young politician—was pleased to lead the campaign for a £125,000 municipal subsidy to the St. Lawrence and Atlantic Railway. Joining Augustin-Norbert Morin, John Rose, Olivier Berthelet, and Benjamin Holmes at a public meeting in Bonsecours Market, Cartier explained that a large municipal subsidy would enable Montrealers to prove that they were not "apathetic," "energyless," and "unenterprising."[100]

This public relations role was accentuated in the 1850s as Cartier became a national leader and ethnic symbol. His nomination as a provisional director between November 1852 and March 1853 gave the Grand Trunk a prominent Montreal French Canadian as a member of its board. *La Minerve* felt that Cartier's ties with the railway brought honour to French Canada. In 1866 Cartier reinforced the company's image by addressing an ecclesiastical dinner held in a St. Jean convent. After acknowledging the supremacy of the sacred over the secular, he described industry as the expression of man's genius and reminded his audience, which included ten bishops, that it was the Grand Trunk that had transported them comfortably to their meeting.[101] He told the first session of the Canadian Parliament that the Grand Trunk had provided "cheap transportation" and had "increased the value of real estate all over the counrty."[102] Other functions on behalf of the company included a trip to England with a director and the president of the Grand Trunk in 1858 and participation in the official opening of the railway's Victoria Bridge a year later.[103]

However, Cartier was always more than a company figurehead. Active in the formation of the railway to the Atlantic, he also understood the significance of a trunk line running west of Montreal. For generations the Montreal commercial community had tried to develop its western hinterland: the fortunes of friends like the Cuvilliers were built on this forwarding trade. Cartier, product of a merchant family and proprietor of a growing commercial law practice, naturally joined his peers in the scramble for railway charters in the St. Lawrence corridor. In 1851–52 two competing schemes emerged for railways from Montreal to Kingston. Cartier was active in both. His name appeared first as a promoter of the Montreal and Kingston Railway, chartered in August 1851. This project was soon challenged by Francis Hincks who had negotiated a trunk-line scheme with the influential British contractors, Peto, Brassey, Jackson and Betts. Amid rumours of Hincks's Grand Trunk plan, Cartier, Luther Holton, Alexander Galt, and Ira Gould hastily opened the Montreal and Kingston Railway company books in March 1852.[104] During the summer, however, Cartier changed companies and in November 1852 his name appeared as a provisional director of the Grand Trunk Railway.[105] Infighting between the two projects was bitter until the government revoked the Montreal and Kingston charter and gave the Grand Trunk the right to build from Montreal to Toronto. Cartier introduced the Grand Trunk bill, led the Hincks forces, and was on his feet throughout a savage four-hour debate.

Cartier's switch was propitious. Rather than being what *Le Pays* described as the "innocent instrument," Cartier had opted for the government-backed line, the railway with access to British capital and the capacity to expand into markets from Maine to Chicago, and the company that would be the dominant industrial force in Montreal until the 1870s.[106] Cartier's reward came quickly. The first meeting of the Canadian board, in July 1853, named him company solicitor for Quebec. A month later his name appeared in the London board's minutes concerning establishment of a transfer office in London. By 1857 his office had received $10,000 in legal fees from the Grand Trunk.[107] The terms of his partnership with François Pominville in 1859 emphasized the importance of Grand Trunk business to his firm. Cartier was to receive only one-fifth of the partnership's general profits but two-thirds of the profits from the Vaudreuil Railway, the Grand Trunk, and its construction company.[108] The Grand Trunk kept a special London account for Cartier, arranged free train travel for his family in Europe, and forwarded funds directly to his wife.[109] Cartier never invested much in Grand Trunk stocks or bonds, a wise measure given their usual value. In 1859 he owned Grand Trunk debentures with a face value of £225. Still in his portfolio when he died, they were evaluated as worthless by his executors.[110]

In addition to his public relations role Cartier acted as the Grand Trunk's political and legal agent. In these capacities he had little part in company direction or management; he was not a member of the important finance committee and, with the exception of land deals, had no company signing powers.[111] Cartier was not a director after the company was formally organized in July 1853 and, except for one occasion in 1859, did not attend board meetings. In the 1850s Canadian directors like Francis Hincks, John Ross, and Alexander Galt worked out policy with the London board and then forwarded instructions to Cartier, as in the case of this memorandum of 1858: "The honorable G. Cartier will please have a formal contract drawn based upon the written memorandum making the general conditions of the contract in every aspect the same as contained in the Quebec and Richmond contract as to character of the line and as to construction thereof."[112]

The Grand Trunk's Quebec agent for two decades, Cartier's firm handled land deals, commutations, property litigations, labour relations, court cases, and inquests. In an early instance, Cartier travelled to Portland, Maine, to arrange transfer of the Atlantic and St. Lawrence Railway.[113] A more complicated case involved high-water running-rights across the waterfront at Levis: in this suit Cartier acted for the Grand Trunk and John A. Macdonald was hired to represent the St. Lawrence Dock Company, the railway's fellow plaintiff and a company in which the Grand Trunk had a substantial investment.[114] Contested seigneurial dues and the commutation of Grand Trunk lands were a recurring source of revenue for Cartier. By the 1860s the hard-pressed Grand Trunk was defaulting on its dividend and interest payments. The most prominent Canadian investors in the railway were the Seminary of Montreal and the British American Land Company, both of which invested £25,000. In 1863 the Grand Trunk recapitalized its debt with the seminary. While Cartier's role is unclear he was certainly active in the settlement of a £25,000 case between his two most important clients. In the same year his law office acted as the railway's inter-mediary with female religious communities in Montreal which had invested in the Grand Trunk. In 1872 the firm was given full power by the London board to settle with the British American Land Company.[115]

Besides commercial work, Cartier's firm represented the Grand Trunk at accident inquests, labour suits, and in strikes. In 1857 it defended the Grand Trunk against charges brought by a worker who had lost his employment as the result of an accident.[116] In 1864 Pomin-ville spent several days at the inquest into a Grand Trunk accident at Beloeil, Quebec, and reported to Cartier that none of the injured immigrants would bring suit against the Grand Trunk. In the same year Cartier intervened on the Grand Trunk's behalf in the bitter strike by Montreal carters against the railway's shipping agent.[117]

Between 1852 and Confederation, Cartier was Grand Trunk spokesman in the assembly. His various duties included controlling committees, dealing with railway matters, responding to requests to publish contracts or shareholder lists, and blocking legislation that would limit passenger fares or force the company to build drawbridges at level-crossings. He was associated with the charters, subsidies, and regulations presented on the Grand Trunk's behalf in almost every session. Since there was no minister of railways, Cartier introduced most bills himself and then as chairman of the assembly's railway committee saw them through committee.[118] Passage through the as-sembly was facilitated after 1857 by his power as house leader.

In 1852 Hincks asked Cartier to introduce the bill granting the Montreal-Toronto route to the Grand Trunk. The bill's liberal financ-ing clauses—providing for sale of Sulpician lands to the Grand Trunk without public announcement, permission for ecclesiatical and munici-pal corporations to invest in the railway, a grant of £3,000 a mile with the possibility of government advances—would characterize Grand Trunk legislation throughout the decade.[119] Two years later Cartier presented the main Grand Trunk charter, uniting six railway companies and a bridge company and authorizing a provincial guarantee of

£2,211,000.[120] By 1856 the railway was unable to pay its contractors and Cartier presented a new Grand Trunk bond issue of £2,000,000 that had preference over provincial bonds. Careful scheduling of third reading of the bill forced supporters of other railways to vote for the government's legislation before receiving their own subsidies. After the stock market crisis of 1857, Grand Trunk shares fell to 40 per cent of par value and company bonds sold at 73 per cent.[121] Despite heavy opposition Cartier succeeded in passing a bill by which the government renounced its right to interest on its bonds or other investments in the railway.

In the 1850s politicians largely succeeded in making Grand Trunk policy synonymous with the national interest. By the end of the decade, however, it was difficult to conciliate political exigencies in the colony with board pressures from London: this made Cartier's double mandate as cabinet minister and company solicitor increasingly complicated. In 1859 Macdonald and Cartier attended a Grand Trunk board meeting in their capacity as attorneys general and approved a further increase in the railway's preferential bond issue. Two years later Cartier leaked information to the company's London broker that the government's postal subsidy would be increased.[122] A substantial bleeding of the public treasury without parliamentary sanction occurred throughout the period. Between 1856 and 1861 the government made extraordinary advances of $4,000,000; the Indian Department lent the railway $400,000 in City of Toronto bonds; in 1861 Cartier explained that an advance of $688,163 and another for $120,000 had been given in an "emergency" situation when the house was not in session.[123] Since it was becoming impossible to obtain further cash subsidies from the government, Grand Trunk officials turned to the possibility of capitalizing their post office and troop-carrying revenues. Thomas Baring sent Cartier two long letters from London and Edward Watkin, the Grand Trunk president, called on Cartier in his Quebec City office and told him the company needed a £500,000 equipment mortgage and permission to move the railway's head office to London. Cartier's 1862 "Reorganization Bill" granted most of the Grand Trunk demands. In 1867 the railway was granted power to issue £500,000 mortgage bonds that would have preference over almost all previously issued bonds.[124]

Cartier also managed the company's dealings with the city of Montreal. Even before becoming company lawyer he had urged city council to take shares in the Grand Trunk's predecessor; if it did not, he warned, the city would become "recreant" and "backward."[125] By the mid-1850s his cabinet post, seat on the Harbour Commission, and his well-placed friends on the bench, Board of Trade, and city council, helped facilitate matters such as harbour access, level-crossing regulations, station-sites, and municipal subsidies. Aside from its influence on local employment and industry, the Grand Trunk was a potent election force in Montreal. Its workers were an important source of votes and election muscle and even constituted a formal militia unit. In 1851 a wary city council asked railway officials and contractors not to use "violence and force" in upcoming elections.[126] When necessary Cartier negotiated directly with city officials. In 1854 Mayor Wolfred Nelson visited Cartier in Quebec City to discuss impending Grand Trunk legislation. The negotiations between company and municipality were settled among friends since Cartier and Nelson had fought together at St. Denis and in 1854 Cartier had supported Nelson's mayoralty candidature against his own father-in-law. Cartier assured the mayor that the Grand Trunk wanted to compromise with the city and that he would personally remove any contentious parts of the bill. While still in office, Nelson, a doctor, was hired by the Grand Trunk to give medicals to its train engineers.[127]

Another of Cartier's political functions was to block what the Grand Trunk manager called "the evils of competition." In Quebec this meant ensuring a Grand Trunk monopoly along the Montreal docks and blocking railways running towards the Ottawa Valley or Quebec City.[128] The North Shore Railway project, promoted by Quebec City entrepreneurs in the 1850s as a means of developing the north shore of the St. Lawrence and of diverting western trade to Quebec City, was an important threat since it would compete directly with the Grand Trunk, its Montreal terminus, and its south shore route to Quebec City. For two decades Cartier's Conservative colleagues, Joseph Cauchon and Hector Langevin, fought for their railway against the economic and political power of the Grand Trunk. Cauchon sat in the Taché cabinet as minister of crown lands until 1857 when he resigned over his failure to get major concessions for his railway. Politicians from the north shore area felt cheated by Cartier's special relationship with the Grand Trunk and opposed his appointment to the cabinet as "the last person in the world" who should be provincial secretary.[129] Cartier's former law student, Hector Langevin, expressed the same sentiments in his Quebec City newspaper.[130]

Grand Trunk politicians had a dozen tactics to obstruct opposing railways. They argued that government funds were only adequate for trunk lines; they quibbled in committee and charged Quebec City with lack of initiative. Foot-dragging and doubletalk were often necessary:

the 1855 Grand Trunk subsidy, Cartier explained to the house, was not to "authorize the company to borrow, but to authorize the Government to loan."[131] The Taché and Cartier governments gave the North Shore entrepreneurs large timber grants but scheduled their bills to follow Grand Trunk subsidy votes. Moreover, the Grand Trunk with its impressive debts and powerful friends had a strong influence on British capital markets. In 1858 Cartier and two Grand Trunk officials went to London, met with Glyn's and Baring's officials, and according to Quebec City promoters blocked North Shore loans on the London market. On his return Cartier urged Langevin to stay in Canada instead of seeking British capital for his railway. Chartered in 1853, the North Shore Railway Company had not laid a single rail when Cartier died twenty years later.

Chapter Five
Conclusion

By the 1870s Cartier's base was being eroded by forces unleashed in part by the legal, educational, landholding, and political structures that he had helped to build. His strength lay in the Seminary of Montreal, the Conservative party, and the Grand Trunk; by 1872 each of these institutions was being challenged in Montreal. The ultramontanes were picking at the Sulpicians' parish empire, exploiting nationalism, and dividing the Conservative party. The Rouges, tempered by time and the need for English-speaking and clerical support, represented a new pragmatic Liberal threat. The Grand Trunk, dominant railway force in Montreal for a generation, was being challenged by the finance capitalists of the Pacific Railway. Cartier's own social group was increasingly heterogeneous as professional and commercial elements broadened to meet the city's new industrial and transportation needs. His bailiwick in old Montreal was being challenged by industries along the Lachine Canal and mills in the east end; the Sulpicians had built their new school in the countryside on Sherbrooke Street, the Grand Trunk railway station was uptown, the Irish church was at the top of Beaver Hall hill, the new cemetery was on the distant slopes of the mountain.

The New Brunswick schools question, the execution of Thomas Scott in the Northwest, the Riel phenomenon, and French-Canadian emigration were dangerous national problems for a politician closely associated with the ideology of western expansion, ethnic harmony, and Confederation.[1] At the local level, his Montreal-East riding was working-class, increasingly Catholic and French, and susceptible to industrial tensions and religious or ethnic demagoguery. The riding demanded attention, a sure hand, and a strong party machine; Cartier was aloof, authoritarian, and distracted by national responsibilities, a new country estate, and an illness that would prove fatal. As Quebec leader of the Conservative party he controlled patronage in much of the province and, although he rarely took his provincial seat, retained a strong influence on the Chauveau government. In 1865 and 1866 he spent months in London during the Confederation discussions, in 1867 he acted for the Sulpicians in Rome, in 1869 he spent five months in England negotiating acquisition of the Northwest. His militia bill of the same year had over one hundred clauses. The Red River crisis added to his burden and it was Cartier who led the debate on the Manitoba Act. In Macdonald's absences, such as during negotiation of the Treaty of Washington, Cartier acted as house leader.

For decades Bishop Bourget had struggled with the Seminary of Montreal and their lawyer. By the 1870s this confrontation had merged into a larger ultramontane resurgence. Encouraged by publication of the doctrine of papal infallibility and the return of the papal zouaves, the ultramontanes pressed for extended clerical influence in matters of state. In April 1871 they published *le programme catholique*, an open declaration of war against pragmatists like Cartier and his gallican allies. The transformation of moral and parish questions into a formal political program to which political candidates were asked to pledge themselves had obvious ramifications for Cartier who faced provincial elections in 1871 and a mandatory federal election a year later. He was forced to abandon plans to run for the provincial seat of Laprairie because of the opposition of local priests; in Beauharnois where he did become candidate he was subjected to strong pressure to sign *le programme catholique*.[2]

The *programmistes* demanded reform of "defective" laws concerning marriage, education, the erection of parishes, and the granting of registers. By 1872 the ultramontane *Nouveau Monde* was running almost daily articles calling on Roman Catholic MPs to do their duty and reminding them of their "conscience." It pointed out to its readers that "the State is subordinate to the Church and it is not permissible for a people to have laws contrary to the laws of the Church."[3] In a strong public statement Bishop Bourget urged federal voters to elect "men capable of defending the rights of religion in every domain."[4] Shortly before the elections of 1872 *Le Nouveau Monde* summarized ultramontane disdain for Cartier:

Quand nous nous rappelons la longue carrière politique de Sir George-Etienne Cartier, le rôle important qu'il a joué depuis bientôt vingt ans, l'influence qu'il a exercée sur nos destinées, nous regrettons d'envisager la triste fin vers laquelle il s'obstine à courir.

Si fidèle au drapeau du parti conservateur, il eût marché droit dans la vie droite, s'il eût adhéré jusqu'au bout aux principes de la nationalité française et du catholicisme dont il s'était constitué le champion; il aurait pu continuer . . . à conduire les affaires du pays. . .

Mais depuis dix ans, il était engagé dans les luttes dangereuses contre l'autorité épiscopale. . . . Il a préféré nous sacrifier, nous catholiques, nous canadiens, à la popularité de Sir John; il a été entraîné par l'appât du pouvoir.[5]

Cartier's political position deteriorated further at the end of 1871 with the formation of the Parti National. The new body, part of a Rouge attempt to attract nationalist and ultramontane support, continued to emphasize safe liberal measures of judicial reform, efficient and cheap government, and an increase in popular control. However, unlike earlier Rouge programs, there was little in the Parti National program to offend the church; its educational reforms and its call for free land and the repatriation of emigrés were perennial ultramontane themes. As part of their moderate approach, party backers founded a newspaper, *Le National*, whose first issue emphasized the role of religion in French Canada. Adopting the approach that Wilfrid Laurier would legitimize five years later, *Le National* differentiated between a religious liberal and a political liberal, the latter acknowledging that society was founded on religion.[6]

To oppose Cartier in Montreal-East the Parti National nominated Louis-Amable Jetté. Member of an ascendant bourgeois group, Jetté, a merchant's son, was admitted to the bar in 1857. After his victory in 1872 and service in Parliament, Jetté served on the Alaska Boundary Tribunal, became lieutenant-governor in 1898, and finally chief justice of Quebec, 1909–11. His standing as a moderate liberal had been confirmed by his resignation from the Institut Canadien in 1858 and his appointment as editor of *L'Ordre*. The Jetté campaign adopted much of the earlier La Fontaine-Cartier ideology and political technique. To appeal to ultramontanes and nationalists, Jetté attacked Cartier's stand on the New Brunswick question; he attracted further clerical support because of his defence of the church in the Guibord affair. While his opponents insisted on federal disallowance of the New Brunswick legislation, Cartier could only express sympathy for Catholics outside Quebec and explain that "the law is hard but it is the law."[7] To attract business support the contradictions in Cartier's railway and economic policy were exploited from every possible angle. Jetté spoke English well and could appeal to business elements who were disenchanted with Cartier's Grand Trunk affiliations. Finally, the Jetté forces undertook a vigorous grassroots campaign to emphasize Cartier's alienation from workers and organized a smooth election machine to control the streets on election day.

The final blow to Cartier's power in Montreal came with the Pacific Railway debate and his confrontation with Hugh Allan in the spring of 1872. Cartier had played an important role in Confederation, the acquisition of the Northwest and the admission of British Columbia, each of which was predicated on economic expansion, a transcontinental state, and a Pacific railway on Canadian soil. As acting prime minister, Cartier received the British Columbia delegation in June 1870, agreed to complete a railway to the Pacific within ten years, and was instrumental in forcing the agreement through caucus.[8] By 1872 the Conservatives could no longer delay chartering a Pacific railway despite the failure of competing Montreal and Toronto syndicates to unite and the refusal of Allan, leading promoter of the Montreal syndicate, to rid himself of American backers.

Allan's bid for a Pacific charter and his pressure on Cartier were part of a transcontinental and transatlantic struggle between his Montreal Ocean Steamship Company and the Grand Trunk. Although the two companies had had a shipping agreement from 1859 to 1869, Allan was fearful of a Grand Trunk monopoly in western trade and its control over freight rates. For its part, the Grand Trunk explored the possibility of developing its own line to the Pacific but—committed to its well-developed American route to the west—finally refused to take shares in Allan's company.[9]

Cartier's Montreal-East riding was particularly vulnerable to attack from the Allan forces. His strength in Montreal lay with two venerable west-end institutions, the seminary and the Grand Trunk. Allan was able to exploit Cartier's gallicanism, his weakness in his east-end working-class constituency, and his subservience to Grand Trunk interests. He hired young francophone professionals resentful of the Cartier clique, and subsidized La Minerve, the Montreal Gazette, and other newspapers that promoted his transportation interests. These newspapers emphasized that his railway terminus in the east end would raise property values and provide jobs. By pressures such as these Allan in his own estimation won over twenty-seven of Cartier's forty-five francophone MPs.[10] In April 1872 and again in June important delegations visited Cartier; they emphasized the importance of a large

Montreal subsidy for Allan's railway and urged Cartier to be less stringent in his restrictions on Allan's Pacific syndicate.

In his use of social and financial resources, Allan was aided by the simmering religious division in Montreal. Many of the francophone businessmen, lawyers, and journalists whom he hired or named to the Canadian Pacific board were ultramontanes known for their alliance with Bishop Bourget. Joseph-Edouard-Lefebvre de Bellefeuille was secretary of the papal zouaves, pamphleteer of ultramontanism, and secretary of several Allan companies. Joseph Cauchon, Quebec City ultramontane, backer of the North Shore Railway and critic of Cartier, appeared on the Canadian Pacific board for a short time. Liaison with the bishop's palace was handled by Antoine Labelle, curé of St. Jérôme, perennial advocate of colonization railways and sometime lobbyist for the bishop in Quebec City. Assiduously cultivated by Allan, Labelle responded by describing the entrepreneur as the "new Hercules."[11] Bishop Bourget released Curé Labelle from his parish duties to campaign for municipal subsidies for Allan's railway. The ultramontane *Nouveau Monde* endorsed Allan's efforts to dredge the ship channel, to build a bridge over the St. Lawrence, and particularly to construct the Pacific railway.[12]

As well as cooperating, subsidizing, and forming loose coalitions with Cartier's bourgeois, nationalist, and ultramontane opponents, Allan exploited regional aspirations and the colonization movement by participating in several railways that competed directly with the Grand Trunk and that could be integrated into the Pacific network. The Canada Central Railway, the Ontario and Quebec Railway, and the North Shore Railway all had strong local public support that was translated into important municipal and provincial subsidies. Allan was also president of the Montreal Colonization Railway which used the promise of cheap firewood, jobs, colonization, and an east-end terminus to win a municipal subsidy of $1,000,000 in April 1872.[13]

Cartier had little leg-room in the face of these attacks. To offset the influence of Bishop Bourget and the ultramontanes Cartier turned to the province's more liberal bishops and the traditional Bleu alliance with the clergy. In contrast to Bourget's rejection of Cartier's position on the New Brunswick schools question, Archbishop Taschereau was more flexible, affirming that each Catholic was free to choose the best means of ameliorating the position of Catholic minorities. Although the Cartier forces retained the support of many parish clergy, the hierarchy was lukewarm. Bishop Larocque (St. Hyacinthe) was neutral, although he leaned to the Bourget position, Bishops Guigues (Ottawa) and Langevin (Rimouski) were strictly neutral.[14]

It was also difficult for Cartier to combat Jetté's contention that he was a stale tory whose Grand Trunk affiliations were contrary to his constituents' interest in the Pacific Railway. With Bright's disease manifesting itself in his kidneys and legs, Cartier's stamina declined. During the early part of the federal campaign of 1872 he was kept in Ottawa by the House of Commons' debates on the Washington Treaty, the New Brunswick schools question, and the Pacific railway charter. His riding organization, financing, and other campaign details were left to four local businessmen: Henry Starnes, former mayor and manager of the Ontario Bank, Peter Murphy, a merchant, Jean-Louis Beaudry, president of the Banque du Peuple, and Victor Hudon, a textile manufacturer.

In the last weeks of the campaign—and too late to save him from defeat—Cartier succumbed. Early in June Cartier apparently agreed that Allan's syndicate could have the Pacific charter on its own terms. Allan wrote his American backers that he had the "pledge" of Cartier and soon after subscribed $85,000 to Cartier's campaign as part of a total of $162,000 which he put at the disposal of the Conservative party.[15] Cartier also had an eleventh-hour reconciliation with Bishop Bourget who, apparently still suspicious of the Rouge backers of Jetté, visited Cartier at home just a week before the election. This latter-day support from the bishop and the Pacific syndicate president was not enough to stop the rot in the Cartier machine which their own ultramontane and railway forces had encouraged during the past year. Cartier's share of the vote dropped from 54 per cent in 1867 to 38 per cent, he did not take a single one of his riding's thirty-nine polls, and he received only 2,007 votes to Jetté's 3,264 (table 6).[16]

At 8:30 a.m. on election day, August 28, Cartier arrived at the political office he had retained in the now-rented family home on Notre Dame Street. Lying on a chesterfield he slept fitfully through the day, worked periodically, and met with his election agents. At ten in the evening, with defeat certain, Cartier thanked supporters gathered in the street, then returned to his dossiers on the militia expedition to the Red River; at 2 a.m. he left with François Pominville. Although Bishop Taché quickly arranged for him to be elected by acclamation in Provencher, Manitoba, Cartier's career was finished. His health was deteriorating rapidly and he spent his last weeks in Canada at his Limoilou estate before leaving for England at the end of September.[17]

Recriminations came quickly. John A. Macdonald felt Cartier had brought on his own defeat by mishandling the railway question and by "sheer obstinacy." Arthur Dansereau, editor of La Minerve, accused

Cartier of ignoring young party workers and of losing control of the Irish and the dockworkers.[18] Others explained the defeat as "treason" or as a victory for the annexationists, the Rouges, or the fanatics of *Le Nouveau Monde*.[19] The clergy were quick to express their regrets. Bishop Bourget again visited Cartier and the bishop of Ottawa expressed his indignation, predicting that the citizens of Montreal would regret "cet acte d'injustice et ingratitude." In his published regrets, Bishop Larocque of St. Hyacinthe described Cartier as "une victime."[20] One hundred priests from the archdiocese of Quebec sent Cartier their regrets. Cartier, sluggish and sick, gave no explanation of his defeat aside from emphasizing that the basis of the Conservative party's strength was its alliance with the clergy: "Le grand Parti conservateur de la Province de Québec doit ses succès passés à son union avec les membres du clergé de toutes les dénominations et ses succès futurs devront dépendre de cette union."[21]

On September 28 Cartier sailed from Quebec City on an Allan steamer, the *Prussian*. The mood was sombre; observers knew Cartier was doomed. During the election campaign he had tired easily and his legs were so swollen that he attended only two public meetings, both of which he addressed sitting down. Macdonald had already told the governor general that Cartier had an "incurable" illness and would not survive a year. Other colleagues, shocked at his appearance, gave him less than six months.[22]

A degenerative disease of the kidneys, Bright's disease was described enigmatically in medical textbooks of the day as an illness in which death could be "delayed."[23] In the early stages, experienced by Cartier in 1871, the feet and ankles swelled after exertion. In later stages the amount of urine increased to as much as a gallon a night, accompanied by frequent wettings, headaches, and other nervous malfunctions. The victim experienced pain from swelling in the hands, loins, and face; convulsions and coma marked the terminal stage. Blood-letting, bed-rest, and a warm climate were favoured treatments. Cartier's London doctor, Sir George Johnson, a Bright's disease specialist and professor at King's College Hospital, was a prominent exponent of a strict milk diet and "hot-air sweating" in which the "water-logged" patient was covered with flannel blankets under which hot air was pumped.[24] This was alternated with large doses of digitalis which worked to diminish inflammation in the kidneys.

In the last months of his life Cartier lived in the Westminster Palace Hotel and then in an apartment at 47 Welbeck Street on Cavendish Square. He kept busy with his Canadian mail, meetings with Colonial

Office officials, and evenings with friends in the Canadian community. His wife and daughters were already living in Europe and arrived in England a month before Cartier; Luce Cuvillier was also present. Since relations with his wife remained strained, the daughters alternated in taking each parent out separately for walks or carriage rides. In their diaries both girls vented their bitterness at the acrimonious family atmosphere, the declining condition of their father—"notre malheureux vieux"—and the continuing parental pressure to find husbands. Christmas was particularly sad: "privacy for a Merry Christmas, la bonne humeur de dogue, no Christmas boxes except those we give ourselves."[25]

In the spring of 1873 Cartier began planning his return to Canada, much to the horror of his daughters who "shuddered" at the thought of his death at sea. He wrote his Ottawa landlord that he would be in Canada at the end of April and in his weekly letters to Macdonald mentioned sailing on May 15, 22, or 29.[26] However, in the third week of May his condition deteriorated. His stomach and chest pain, bowel inflammation, and feebleness worsened and a week before the end he got out of bed for the last time. Four days later, too weak to write, he dictated his last letter to Macdonald. He died at 6 a.m. on Tuesday, May 20.

> That night he slept which was unusual of late and towards dawn Mamma who had been by his bedside all night left the room for a few minutes with some of the attendants. On her returning a change had occurred and she gave the alarm. Doctors and clergymen were called and all was over within twenty minutes. He rallied strength and told us himself "I am dying."[27]

John Rose arranged a requiem mass in London's French chapel and chose an undertaker of "great skill and respectability" who assured Rose that the embalmed body would "reach Canada in such a condition as his friends would wish."[28] On May 29 Cartier's hermetically sealed coffin was shipped from Liverpool aboard Allan's steamer, the *Prussian*.

Eleven days later the *Prussian* arrived off Quebec City where Cartier's body was transferred to the government steamer *Druid* and, in the presence of Grand Vicar Langevin, placed in a new coffin. Made of polished oak with brass handles the coffin was garnished with wreaths inscribed "A mon mari" and "A mon père" and a third from his valet marked "A mon maître et ami."[29] After a requiem mass by Grand Vicar Cazeau, members of the public were allowed on board to pay their respects. In the evening the coffin, accompanied by cannon salutes every minute and music from two bands, was transported up the hill to the basilica for funeral prayers chanted by Archbishop Taschereau. The following day, with Cartier's mother-in-law and brother Antoine-Côme on board, the *Druid* left for Three Rivers where the coffin was carried to the cathedral for another mass. As the steamer passed Sorel, Berthier, and Cartier's estate at Longue Pointe, flags flew at half-mast and church bells were rung. From another steamer the governor general's wife saw the *Druid*: "When we were at tea we heard some music—the Dead March—being played and looking out we saw, passing slowly in the darkness, the steamer with the body of Sir George Cartier on board; it was a striking moment—the chapel on board lighted up, the band playing and bells tolling at sea, answered by bells tolling on shore."[30]

In Montreal the body lay in state for two days in the lawyers' library in the courthouse. At 8:30 a.m. on Friday, June 13, the coffin was placed on a special hearse built at a cost of $2,000. Covered in silver silk and displaying at both ends Cartier's coat of arms, the twenty-two-foot-high, gothic-style hearse was drawn by eight horses, each tended by a groom attired in black capes. The funeral procession took a long, circular route from the courthouse to the church, along Bon-secours, St. Denis, and Ste. Catherine streets before going down St. Lawrence to Notre Dame Church. Many of the 50,000 to 100,000 people who lined the route wore mourning badges of silver ribbon and rosettes with a photograph of Cartier. Houses, institutions, and public buildings were decorated for the occasion: observers were particularly impressed by the Sisters of Notre Dame convent, Louis Sénécal's home, the post office, and city hall. The hearse was preceded by the infantry, the militia, literary institute and artisan representatives, civil servants, mayors, members of the Board of Trade, Harbour Commission, Wheat Board, and, immediately preceding the hearse, members of the national societies. Noted in the procession were the English Workingmen's Society, St. Bridget's Temperance and Irish Benevolent Society, the Stonecutters' Association, the First Cavalry Troop, the Fire Brigade, and cadets from the Montreal High School. Pallbearers included Lieutenant-Governor Howland of Ontario, Judge Louis Sicotte, A. A. Dorion, Sir Francis Hincks, and Sir Alexander Galt; Sir John A. Macdonald and all but two members of his cabinet attended the service. Since Cartier's wife and daughters had remained in England, his brother, Antoine-Côme Cartier, was the closest family member in the procession.[31]

At Notre Dame church the coffin was placed on a fourteen-foot bier around which burned 500 candles. Over the bier was a three-storey, forty-foot tower topped by four funeral busts of Cartier and a golden cross. The church was decorated with purple crepe; on the wall opposite the bier hung a large, blue silk banner speckled with silver tears and dominated by a beaver surrounded by maple leaves. In his will Cartier had asked that his funeral mass be chanted by the Sulpician Superior, Abbé Bayle. However, Bishop Bourget, whose long memory was reflected in a *Nouveau Monde* editorial stating that Cartier had been guilty of "persecution mesquine" in the parish question, insisted that Cartier's ultramontane brother-in-law, Bishop Fabre, celebrate the mass.[32] Bayle did receive the body into the church and the Sulpicians' 300-voice boys' choir sang during the service.

En route to Côte des Neiges cemetery the funeral procession stopped briefly before the Beaver Hall Hill home of Cartier's former law partner, Judge Berthelot. The final ceremony was short since Bishop Bourget had not authorized eulogies by clerics; secular leaders like Macdonald and Premier Chauveau followed suit and refrained from graveside eulogies. By 5 p.m. carriages were carrying the dignitaries back down the mountain into Montreal.

Tied to a specific mid-nineteenth-century milieu, Cartier, in his family, life-style, social ambitions, politics, and professional and business interests, serves as one barometer of the Montreal bourgeois experience. Raised during the long agricultural crisis in Lower Canada and a witness to the collapse of his family's grain business and the bankruptcy of his father, Cartier chose to become a Montreal lawyer. The move to Montreal did not weaken his ties with the merchant community and his marriage gave his early career an important boost. Although he developed sharp differences with his wife's family, cursing them in his will and betraying them in his bed, after his death form and family again became important. His mother-in-law accompanied the coffin from Quebec City to Montreal; his ultramontane brother-in-law celebrated the funeral mass. Even his concubine was a member of the Montreal bourgeoisie.

The separation of classes in Montreal was reinforced by institutional and spatial factors. Although he nurtured an image as French Canada's "representative man," Cartier had little contact with the lower levels of his society aside from domestic servants and hired help. Housed, supervised, and taught for seven years by an élite corps of French priests, he and his peers shared a common classroom, dormitory, and ideological experience. This isolation from other classes was perpetuated in the old

Cartier in his prime, 1853

Cartier in declining health, 1871

central part of Montreal where Cartier lived and worked in a milieu of businessmen, clerics, and fellow professionals. His friends were local politicians, merchants, and speculators; his law practice, property investments, school, church, and homes were all located within a fifteen-block area.[33] For years he lived in Rasco's Hotel which also contained the offices of the town major with whom he negotiated the rental of his St. Paul street building as a military hospital. In this milieu even national organizations like the St. Jean Baptiste Society had a high degree of social group isolation.[34]

This isolation was more spatial and social than ethnic. Cartier had a facility for working with English-speaking leaders and cooperated easily with Lewis Drummond, John Rose, and even George Brown; colleagues like Alexander Galt called on him to arrange personal loans.[35] After 1853 Cartier made English entries in his legal accounts and his spoken English, although always accented, became increasingly fluent. Aware of the anglophone minority's political power in Montreal, he made important concessions in education legislation and in the terms of Confederation.

Until the last years of his life Cartier adapted effectively to the changing conditions of nineteenth-century capitalism. A Montreal resident for forty-eight years, he was no stranger to bankruptcy, strikes, and urban violence. Nor did his ethnic origins restrict his geographic mobility. From the age of ten he lived in a school residence and then in hotels until his marriage at thirty-two. In his middle years he adjusted easily to the rotation of the political capital between Toronto and Quebec City and thrived in the masculine, extrafamilial, and interethnic world of the Canadian politician. As a lawyer he built a general practice into an influential business whose corporate clients included the government of France, the city's most important religious community, and various railway, mining, and insurance companies. He supplemented his law and political revenues with property investments that returned substantial rents. By the 1860s he was placing his surplus capital in bank and, to a lesser extent, industrial stocks.

Cartier's visible wealth kept pace with this economic evolution. Fourth-generation offspring of a merchant family with large homes, servants, military commissions, and fine silver, he moved easily into a Montreal world of pianos, Italian restaurants, and private railway coaches. His rental, legal, political, and patronage income enabled him to maintain an impressive home, library, and wine cellar. Hired help permitted him to live in isolation from daily preoccupations. Servants, a housekeeper, and a gardener performed domestic duties in his Ottawa,

Cartier's funeral cortège before the Grand Trunk offices on St. James Street, Montreal, June 13, 1873

Montreal, and country residences, and his valet travelled with him. Repair, rental, and management of his investment properties was delegated to his contractor, law partner, or financial adviser. Junior clerks and political secretaries administered his law, cabinet, and riding offices. Towards the end of his life he developed imperial ambitions that drew him towards the British metropolis. Adopting the clothes, lifestyle, and status symbols of the British élite, he expressed a desire to settle in London. Proud of his title, coat-of-arms, and uniforms, he dabbled in exotic travel books, classical sculpture, and saddlery.

Cartier began his political career as representative of a rural riding which his grandfather had represented and which contained the family estate and the graves of his parents. Although he continued to pay ritual tribute to rural Quebec, Cartier, his friends, his work, and his ethic were urban and capitalist. Winning a city riding, however, proved difficult, and in Montreal he was defeated three times. A generation of mutual baiting and bad blood with the Rouges, his alliance with gallican forces, and his twenty-year opposition to railways with a terminus in east-end Montreal increased his vulnerability. From the late 1850s onward Cartier had country-wide responsibilities as (at one time or another) attorney general, prime minister, minister of militia, and negotiator in Britain. These functions forced the often-absent member for Montreal-East to rely on traditional sources of power: the church, party, patronage, and employers.

In the first stage of his career Cartier acted for his elders as songwriter for national festivals, secretary of *patriote* committees, gun-runner in 1837, campaign organizer in Montreal. By the 1850s he had inherited La Fontaine's law partner, clerical clients, and political mantle and was a central figure in providing the bourgeoisie with the political tools for the transportation revolution and in establishing centralized, rationalized, and bureaucratized political, social, and legal structures. Both in his personal behaviour and in political acts such as the formation of the militia he showed a consistent concern for working-class discipline. Industrialization, urbanization, and accompanying social control mechanisms—notably bourgeois values and new political, educational, judicial, and fraternal institutions—brought persistent, if disorganized, popular protest. The choice of a "safe" political capital, the structuring of local transportation, taxation, and administrative facilities, strong reaction to the school taxes rebellion, strikes, and urban riots provide ample evidence of class conflict. Cartier's role in the transformation of the elementary school system, the provision of provincial police, regional courthouses and jails, the tightening of parish record-keeping systems, the growth of savings banks, and the neutralization of national societies reflects his interest in controlling the proletariat. He modelled the St. Jean Baptiste Society on the Roman legion and encouraged companies like the Grand Trunk Railway to form company militia units; his militia bill of 1868 gave military authorities the right to search houses arbitrarily and force citizens to perform military service.[36]

As the dominant Quebec politician during the 1850s and 1860s Cartier mediated between his society and outside interests, thereby performing one of the classic functions of a colonial élite. It was a role of particular importance in the Montreal region—an area with a preindustrial landholding system, an established Catholic Church, eighteenth-century judicial and social structures, and a large, propertyless rural and urban proletariat. Cartier and his allies had sufficient political power to force the rapid transformation of a society permeated by feudal and *ancien régime* structures. They imposed freehold tenure, a modern civil code, a federal political structure, and a universal educational system and assured the legitimization of these fundamental institutions among an often hostile Quebec populace.[37]

This extension of bourgeois power was carried out in systematic fashion despite the apparent political confusion of the Union period. Seigneurial tenure had to be abolished before the revised civil code could be applied. In turn, Cartier was anxious to complete revision of the civil code before Confederation. An attempt was made to integrate and coordinate administrative and institutional structures. The implementation of regional judicial and educational bureaucracies necessitated improved means of transportation. Municipalities and religious corporations were given revised civil status and were empowered to borrow to promote local economic development.

In fulfilling these functions Cartier always had important social and economic assistance from other elements in the élite who understood his significance. The British government rented his premises, awarded him a much-wanted baronetcy, and flattered him socially at the highest levels of the aristocracy and monarchy. Cartier earned this trust by steadfast loyalty after 1838, by his opposition to the annexation movement of 1849 and other manifestations of pro-Americanism, by his deep commitment to British constitutional principles, by his insistence on a strong Canadian defence force, and by his efforts to direct French-Canadian nationalism into established political channels. By the late 1860s Cartier—colonial and (despite the Grand Trunk) largely mercantile in orientation—was being eclipsed by the rise of a national and industrial bourgeoisie. His increasing attachment to British life, his isolation from both his peers and his constituents, and his defeat in 1872—partly as the result of the opposition of Bishop Bourget, finance capitalists like Hugh Allan, and young "national" bourgeois like Jetté—provide tentative evidence of this fractionalism.

In his relations with the Seminary of Montreal, Cartier was student, lawyer, and parishioner. Essentially a French religious community despite their 200-year-old presence in Quebec, the Sulpicians felt threatened by Canadian secular and clerical forces. Cartier, never anti-clerical like many of his peers, imitated the examples of La Fontaine and the Colonial Office and gave the Sulpicians security. Indifferent to religion in a spiritual sense, he praised the social role of Catholicism and defended the seminary against the bishop and other French-Canadian clerical opponents. His most important service for the seminary was to arrange the special legislation transforming their seigneurial holdings into freehold tenure. This resolved the conflict between the seminary and the expansionist, free-market Montreal bourgeoisie, it enabled the Sulpicians to continue their social functions, and facilitated the channelling of their landed wealth into mortgages, transportation stocks, and other forms of capitalist investment.

The Montreal commercial community appreciated Cartier's role in erecting "conservatory barriers" (the revised civil code) and in achieving a "social revolution . . . at a trivial cost" (freehold tenure).[38] Emphasizing economic development, social stability, and a centralized, hierarchical state, business, church, and ethnic leaders used Cartier as their agent and intermediary in imposing their largely harmonious class interests. His political conservatism, exemplified by his emphasis on an appointed upper house, the open ballot, Confederation, the military, and the monarchy, provided important guarantees of order and authority. He legitimized property by linking it to nationalism, the soil, and "progress"; socialist critics of property were dismissed as "blasphemers."[39] His positions as cabinet minister, harbour commissioner, and chairman of the railway committee and his influence with the party oligarchy, the caucus, and the Chauveau government enabled him to supervise legislation relating to municipalities, interest rates, subsidies, charters, bills of exchange, mortgage law, port facilities, and roads. The Grand Trunk was a special case. Its lawyer for twenty years, Cartier stage-managed its annual government loans, defended it at accident inquests, arranged its postal subsidies, and stalled its competitors. Although the railway was increasingly British in its financing and American in its traffic, and had regional interests antithetical to those of important parts of Quebec, Cartier endeavoured, with some success, to make the Grand Trunk synonymous with national pride. Not surprisingly, he was named to bank, mining, insurance, and railway boards, employed to handle legal and lobbying matters, and financed in his political campaigns.

Cartier was liberally rewarded for his political, institutional, and ideological role as "legitimizer" and "mediator." If he had to borrow money in 1868 to pay the costs of becoming "Sir George," the problem was one of cash flow rather than of real wealth for he had the means to indulge his taste for travel, champagne, fruit trees, coats-of-arms, and servants.[10] He visited England almost every year after 1865 and bought a country estate in Canada in 1869. Two years later he could afford to support his daughters and estranged wife in Europe. This private world appears to have been more anxious and insecure than the world of political and ideological certainties he inhabited in public. His stated commitment to his Montreal constituency, to a new political nationality, to French Canada and its roots, and to social order and stability, seems to be contradicted by his persistent anglophilism, by his rush for status, by his rejection of accepted family life for a long-term, extraconjugal relationship, and by his replacement of the urban bourgeois experience with that of the country gentleman.

In any case, his life was almost over. Rejected by the voters of Montreal-East, implicated in the Pacific scandal, and stricken with a slow, debilitating illness, he spent the last seven months of his life in London in the milieu he had come to love best: Luce Cuvillier, many of his Montreal friends and associates, the Westminster Palace Hotel, the Colonial Office, the clubs, and the best doctors were all there. Although he wanted to go home to die, his death in the imperial capital fitted his role. His national function was recognized in the theatrical rites of his state funeral in Montreal.

Chronology

	FAMILY	PERSONAL RESIDENCE	TRAVEL	LAW PRACTICE
1735	Jacques Cartier I emigrates to Quebec			
1770	Jacques Cartier II settles in St. Antoine			
1776 –83	Jacques Cartier II aids British			
1782		Construction of "House of Seven Chimneys"		
1800	Cartiers inaugurate mail service, Sorel to St. Hyacinthe			
1805				
1808				
1814	March: Jacques Cartier II dies leaving capital of £166,370. Sept. 6: George-Etienne Cartier born	Family home, St. Antoine		
1824	Enters Collège de Montréal			
1830	Cartier's mother sues his father for bankruptcy	Boards at private school, Montreal		
1831				Law student, office of E.E. Rodier
1834				
1835				Nov.: called to bar Opens law office with brother Damien
1836				
1837		Nov. 17: flees Montreal Nov. 17–22: at family home, St. Antoine Nov. 23–Dec. 1: in hiding near St. Denis		
1838		Dec.-May: in hiding near St. Antoine May–late 1838: in Plattsburgh, N.Y. and Burlington, Vt.	May 17: enters United States at Rouses Point Late 1838: returns to Montreal	
1839				Early 1839: resumes law practice with brother Damien at 3 St. Vincent St.
1840	Mother's bankruptcy suit against his father renewed			Dec.: Damien leaves partnership
1841	Death of father			

PROFESSIONAL		AWARDS & OFFICES	HISTORICAL EVENTS
INVESTMENTS	POLITICS		
			American Revolution
	Jacques Cartier II elected to assembly for Surrey, 1805–9		
		Jacques Cartier II, lieutenant-colonel, Verchères militia	
		Jacques Cartier III, lieutenant and paymaster, later major, Verchères militia	War of 1812–14
	Student rebellions at Collège de Montréal	Jacques Cartier III, lieutenant-colonel, Verchères militia	
	Participates in St. Jean Baptiste celebrations Campaigns for Nelson and Papineau		Ninety-Two Resolutions
	Secretary, Central Committee for district of Montreal		
	May: co-secretary of Permanent Central Committee Sept. 5: attends organizational meeting of Fils de la Liberté Nov. 22: joins rebellion at St. Denis		Nov.–Dec.: rebellions in Lower and Upper Canada
	June: Cartier, La Fontaine, and Papineau meet in Saratoga, N.Y. Sept. 20: sends loyalty oath to British authorities		May: Lord Durham arrives in Canada Nov.: renewed rebellion Dec. 1838–Feb. 1839: execution of 12 *patriotes*
	Nov. 6: attends governor's levée		Sept.: deportation of 58 *patriotes*
			Crown recognizes Sulpician property rights Ignace Bourget becomes Bishop of Montreal
Parents give Cartier 1,200 acres in Wolfe County	Refuses to run for assembly Mar.–Apr.: campaigns for La Fontaine in Terrebonne Sulpicians employ La Fontaine as lawyer		Union Act takes effect

	PERSONAL			
	FAMILY	RESIDENCE	TRAVEL	LAW PRACTICE
1842		Rasco's Hotel		
1843				
1844				
1845				
1846	June 16: marries Hortense Fabre			First railway case
1847	Birth of daughter Josephine	Donnegana's Hotel		
1848	Apr. 23: death of mother	Moves to 16 Notre Dame St.	Visits Boston	Moves law office to 26 St. Vincent St.
1849	Birth of daughter Hortense			
1850				
1851		Assembly sits in Quebec City 16 Notre Dame St.		Dec.: named Queen's Counsel
				Acts for Richelieu Co.
1852				
1853	Birth of daughter Reine-Victoria	Assembly sits in Toronto		Appointed to examination committee, Montreal Bar Association Named Montreal lawyer for Grand Trunk Railway Forms partnership with Berthelot
1854	July: death of daughter Reine-Victoria and father-in-law in cholera epidemic			
1855		Assembly sits in Quebec City		
1856				
1857		Assembly sits in Toronto		Acts as lawyer for Cuvilliers

PROFESSIONAL		AWARDS & OFFICES	HISTORICAL EVENTS
INVESTMENTS	POLITICS		
Buys corner of Notre Dame and Bonsecours streets			
Constructs first building		Secretary, St. Jean Baptiste Society	
	Manages Drummond's campaign Apr.: counsel at inquest on Haymarket election riot		
Buys St. Paul Street property			Abolition of British Corn Laws
Leases St. Paul St. property as military hospital	Campaigns for municipal subsidy for railway to Portland, Me.	Honorary director, Montreal City and District Savings Bank	
Constructs two buildings, St. Paul St.		Director, National Loan Fund Life Assurance Co. Captain, Montreal Voltigeurs militia	Heavy Irish immigration
	Apr.: elected to assembly for Verchères in by-election Duel with Joseph Doutre Supports free trade	President, managing committee, Montreal Advocates Library	Mar.: Baldwin-La Fontaine ministry formed Revolutions in Europe
	Feb.–Mar.: votes for Rebellion Losses Bill Oct.: organizes loyalty petition, opposes annexation Introduces petitions for St. Lawrence and Atlantic Railway and St. Jean Baptiste Society	Director, Canada Life Assurance Co.	Apr. 25: Elgin signs Rebellion Losses Bill Burning of Parliament Annexation movement Rebellion against education measures (1849–50)
		Vice-president, St. Jean Baptiste Society	
	Declines solicitor-generalship Re-elected Verchères		Great Exhibition, London Upper Canada's population exceeds Lower Canada's
	Chairman, Railway Committee of assembly (1852–67). Sept.: declines portfolio of commissioner of public works	Nov. 1852–May 1853: provisional director, Grand Trunk Railway (Montreal to Toronto)	July: great fire of Montreal
	Introduces charter for Grand Trunk Railway	Director, Canada Loan Co.	June 9: Gavazzi religious riots in Montreal St. Lawrence and Atlantic Railway opened to Portland
	Mar.: supports Nelson against father-in-law in mayoralty campaign June: re-elected Verchères Sept.: nomination as speaker defeated	President, St. Jean Baptiste Society Commissioner, Paris Exposition (1854–55)	Reciprocity treaty with U.S. Nov: abolition of seigneurial tenure
Buys lot on Notre Dame St.	Jan: named provincial secretary Montreal harbour commissioner (1855–56)	Awarded LL.D. by Collège de St. Jean	
	May: named attorney general	Director, Montreal Mining Co.	Lower Canadian education reforms passed
	Dec.: defeated in Montreal but re-elected Verchères		Judicial reforms passed Civil code commission established First Cartier-Macdonald ministry

	PERSONAL		LAW PRACTICE
	FAMILY	RESIDENCE	TRAVEL	

	FAMILY	RESIDENCE	TRAVEL	LAW PRACTICE
1858			Oct.–Nov.: trip to London, Paris	
1859		Assembly sits in Quebec City 20 Notre Dame St.		Berthelot raised to bench Forms partnership with Pominville
1860	(circa) Liaison with Luce Cuvillier begins	Assembly sits	Oct.: visits Boston	
1861		in Toronto		
1862				Betournay joins partnership
1863		Assembly sits in Quebec City	Jan.: meets Lincoln in Washington	Law office moved to 31 St. Vincent St.
1864				
1865	Brother Damien dies		April 6–July 6: London, Paris	Lawyer for European Assurance Co.
1866	Nov.: writes new will	Ottawa becomes official residence	Nov. 12, 1866–May 16, 1867: London, Paris, Rome	Honorary member, Upper Canadian bar Pleads for Sulpicians in Rome Firm acts for French government
1867			Sept.–Oct.: Naples and Paris	
1868			Oct. 3, 1868–Apr. 15, 1869: London, Paris	
1869		Buys country home ("Limoilou")		
1871	First symptoms of Bright's disease Dec: wife and daughters leave for Europe	Ottawa and "Limoilou"		$1,000 retainer from Sulpicians
1872			Sept. 27: leaves for England	
1873	May 1: brother-in-law named bishop May 20: Cartier dies in London June 13: state funeral in Montreal			
1886	Death of Josephine Cartier			
1898	Death of Lady Cartier			
1900	Death of Luce Cuvillier			
1941	Death of Hortense Cartier			

PROFESSIONAL		AWARDS & OFFICES	HISTORICAL EVENTS
INVESTMENTS	POLITICS		
	Aug. 6: named inspector general	Director, Transatlantic	Aug. 6–7: double shuffle
	Aug. 7: named attorney general	Telegraph Co.	
	Aug. 7: accepts principle of federation		
	Montreal harbour commissioner (1858–59)		
	Presents seigneurial legislation for		Nov.: opening of Victoria
	Sulpicians		Bridge
			Choice of Ottawa as capital
			July: Prince of Wales visits
			Canada
	July: elected Verchères, defeated Montreal-East		
Buys buildings on	May: resigns as attorney general after defeat		Fall of Macdonald-Cartier
Notre Dame St.	on militia bill		government
Clara Symes lends	June: re-elected Montreal-East	Director, British North	Sulpicians and bishop appeal
Cartier $10,000		American Life	to Rome over division of
		Association of Scotland	parish
Constructs two	Mar.: named attorney general	Nov.: Mme Cartier	June 30: formation of
buildings on Notre	Accepts representation by population and	named godmother of bells	coalition government
Dame St.	federation terms	in Notre Dame Church	Sept. 1–8: Charlottetown
Buys 200 acres of	Re-elected Montreal-East		Conference
crown land, Wolfe			Oct. 10–26: Quebec Conference
County			
Substantial bank		Director, Rideau Club,	Confederation negotiations
and stock invest-		Ottawa	in London
ments begin			
Cuvillier and Co.	Apr.: refuses chief justiceship		First transatlantic cable
handle			London conference
investments			Revised civil code takes effect
	July: named minister of militia and defence	July: refuses Companion	July: Confederation
	Sept.: elected Montreal-East (provincial and	of Order of Bath	
	federal seats)		
	Mar.: introduces Militia Bill	Apr.: receives baronetcy	
	Negotiates Hudson's Bay purchase		
	May: introduces Hudson's Bay resolutions		First Riel uprising
	July: elected for provincial seat of		Publication of *programme*
	Beauharnois		*catholique*
	Nov.: presents bill for admission of British		New Brunswick School Act
	Columbia to Confederation		
	May 7: presents Canadian Pacific Railway Bill		
	Aug. 28: defeated Montreal-East		
	Sept. 14: elected Provencher, Man.		
			Apr.: Pacific scandal
			charges raised in Parliament
			Nov.: resignation of
			Macdonald government

Abbreviations

ANQ	Archives Nationales du Québec, Quebec
ASSM	Archives du Séminaire Saint-Sulpice, Montreal
Best	Henry Best, "George-Etienne Cartier" (Ph.D., Laval University, 1969)
Boyd	John Boyd, *Sir George Etienne Cartier* (Toronto: Macmillan, 1914)
DCB	*Dictionary of Canadian Biography* (Toronto: University of Toronto Press, 1965–)
DCP	Papers, Dr. George-Etienne Cartier, Montreal
Discours	Joseph Tassé, *Discours de Sir George Cartier* (Montreal, 1893)
Fees Book	Professional Fees Account Book of George-Etienne Cartier, 1835–53, Public Archives of Canada, M.G.23, Société Numismatique, series B, microfilm M 869
Hortense Cartier diary	Diary of Hortense Cartier, Archives of the Archbishop of Montreal, Montreal
Josephine Cartier diary	Diary of Josephine Cartier, Archives of the Archbishop of Montreal, Montreal
McCord	Cartier Collection, McCord Museum, Montreal
PAC	Public Archives of Canada, Ottawa
RHAF	*Revue d'histoire de l'Amérique française*
Sweeny	Alastair Sweeny, *George-Etienne Cartier: A Biography* (Toronto: McClelland and Stewart, 1976)

Notes

Notes to Introduction

1. W.L. Morton, *The Critical Years: The Union of British North America, 1857–73*, (Toronto: McClelland and Stewart, 1964), p. 65; J.I. Cooper, "The Political Ideas of George-Etienne Cartier," *Report*, Canadian Historical Association (1938); pp. 286–94; Pierre Berton, *The National Dream* (Toronto: McClelland and Stewart, 1971), p. 75; Sweeny, p. 113.

2. See, for example, the examination of Cartier's role in Canada-United States relations in Robin Winks, *Canada and the United States: The Civil War Years* (Baltimore: Johns Hopkins Press, 1960), pp. 40–41, 239–40, 315–16; see also A. I. Silver, "Quebec and the French-speaking Minorities, 1864–1917" (Ph.D. thesis, University of Toronto, 1973); Silver, "French Canada and the Prairie Frontier," *Canadian Historical Review* 50, no.1, (March 1969): 11–36; G. F. G. Stanley, *The Birth of Western Canada* (Toronto: University of Toronto Press, 1960).

Notes to Chapter One

1. B. Pontbriand, *Mariages de Saint-Antoine sur Richelieu, 1741–1965* (Sillery: published by author, 1966), p.1; J. B. A. Allaire, *Histoire de la paroisse de Saint-Denis sur Richelieu* (St. Hyacinthe: *Courrier de Saint-Hyacinthe*, 1905); Soeur de Saint-Joseph de Saint-Hyacinthe, *La petite histoire de chez nous* (St. Hyacinthe: Historical Society of St. Hyacinthe, 1938), 38:45.

2. DCP, contrat de vente, M. Noisseau to Jacques Cartier dit Langevin, February 19, 1762.

3. Boyd, p.414; Richard Rice pointed out to me that in 1825 the Cartiers owned a schooner built at St. Ours and the 118-ton schooner *Abeona* built at Chambly. Registers of Quebec, no. 50, n.d.

4. DCP, Charles Duval account for £120 to Jacques Cartier, January 28, 1802; Boyd, p.412; Notarial Archives of Montreal, L.H. Latour, notary, no.910, testament de Jacques Cartier, June 9, 1811; L. H. Latour, notary, no.911, vente publique des affaires de Jacques Cartier, April 18, 1814. Jacques Cartier II's career, social aspirations, and economic standing had much in common with other south-shore merchants. See, for example, Alan Dever's biographies of Jean-Baptiste Raymond and Pierre-Guillaume Guérout in *DCB*, vol. 6 (forthcoming).

5. DCP, list of Cartiers in militia service, n.d.

6. Ibid., indenture form, Joseph Paradis, n.d. (in his indenture oath Paradis contracted not to "haunt taverns or playhouses"); licence for a shopkeeper to retail liquors, 1790; Jean-Jacques Lefebvre, "L'aïeul maternel de Sir George-Etienne Cartier: Joseph Paradis, 1732–1802," *RHAF* 14 (1960): 472–74; parish records, presbytery of St. Antoine.

7. Boyd, p.417; in his will Jacques Cartier II forgave his nephew a £2,000 debt, left him £23,000 and rented him his buildings and animals for six years. Notarial Archives of Montreal, L. H. Latour, notary, no.910, testament de Jacques Cartier, January 9, 1811.

8. McCord, Jacques Cartier III to Governor Dalhousie, December 27, 1827; Cartier used the title of lieutenant-colonel in the census of 1831, *Census of 1831*, St. Antoine (Surrey), p.2032.

9. Fernand Ouellet, *Le Bas Canada 1791–1840: Changements structuraux et crise* (Ottawa: University of Ottawa Press, 1976), pp.282–83; Boyd, p.413. Thirty-nine litres equal one minot. *Census of Canada* 1870–71, 1:42.

10. Notarial Archives of Montreal, L. H. Latour, notary, no.910, testament de Jacques Cartier, June 9, 1811; no.911, vente publique des affaires de Jacques Cartier, April 18, 1814.

11. DCP, Court of King's Bench, Montreal, June 1840, Requête de Dame Marguerite Paradis.

12. DCP, bill from *La Minerve*, October 1841; bill from fabrique de St. Antoine, October 18, 1841; *Census of 1831*, St. Antoine (Surrey), p.2032.

13. Boyd, p.415.

14. "George" without an "s" is clear from his baptismal record, parish register, St. Antoine presbytery. Cartier's godmother was his aunt, Claire Paradis. There is no record of a school in St. Antoine until 1829 or in neighbouring Contrecoeur before 1826. Soeur de Saint-Hyacinthe, *La petite histoire de chez nous*, p.148; however, L. O. David, *Biographies et portraits* (Montreal: Beauchemin et Valois, 1876) and Boyd, p.21, both mention Cartier's attendance at a local school.

15. The Cartiers may have been unable to pay the school fees of their children. Ten years after his graduation Cartier paid off the outstanding school bills for his brother Damien and himself. DCP, receipt from économe du Petit Séminaire, February 25, 1842.

16. Olivier Maurault, *Le Collège de Montréal, 1767–1967* (Montreal: Antonio Dansereau, 1967).

17. ASSM, tiroir 47, no.75, prospectus for Collège de Montréal, 1826, p.3.

18. Ibid., no.50, J. G. Rogue, Règlement du Petit Séminaire de Montréal, 1806—28, p.10.

19. This strictness did not prevent student smoking. Towards the end of his life Cartier remarked that he had smoked until the age of thirteen and never after. *Discours*, August 16, 1871, p.711.

20. ASSM, tiroir 47, no.83, clipping from *L'Observateur*, November 13, 1830.

21. Maurault, *Le Collège de Montréal*, p.125.

22. Boyd, p.20; McCord, Prix obtenus par Sir George Cartier. . ., handwritten note, n.d.

23. *Discours*, April 16, 1866, p.483.

24. J. P. Bernard, P. A. Linteau, and J. C. Robert, "La structure professionnelle de Montréal en 1825," *RHAF* 30, no.3 (December 1976):412.

25. For treatment of the rebellions and the bourgeoisie, see Alfred Dubuc, "Problems in the Study of the Stratification of Canadian Society, 1769—1840," in Michiel Horn and Ronald Sabourin, eds., *Studies in Canadian Social History* (Toronto: McClelland and Stewart, 1974), p.128, and particularly Ouellet, *Le Bas Canada, 1791—1840*, p.275.

26. Gérard Filteau, *Histoire des patriotes* (Montreal: L'Aurore, 1975), p.117.

27. Robert Rumilly, *Histoire de Montréal* (Montreal: Fides, 1970), 2:209.

28. *La Minerve*, September 18, 1837.

29. Elinor Kyte Senior, *The Rebellions in Lower Canada, 1837—38: And the British Military Response* (Ottawa: Canadian War Museum, forthcoming), chap. 6; Archives de la compagnie de Saint-Sulpice à Paris, dossier 22, clipping from *L'Ami du Peuple*, December 20, 1837. Joseph Cartier, probably Cartier's uncle, took an oath of allegiance on December 21, 1837.

30. Montreal *Herald*, November 21, 1837, cited in Best, p.45.

31. David, *Biographies et Portraits*, p.149; Rumilly, *Histoire de Montréal*, 2:235—38.

32. Cartier's death is cited in *L'Ami du Peuple*, December 23, 1837, clipping in dossier 22, Archives de la compagnie de Saint-Sulpice à Paris; *La Minerve*, June 22, 1873.

Notes to Chapter Two

1. DCP, Paul Montannary, huissier bills to Cartier, 1836—37.

2. Fees Book.

3. Best, p.124; Fees Book, Aimé Massue entries.

4. McCord, clipping from *Times and Daily Commercial Advertiser*, April 24, 1844; J.P. Bernard, P.A. Linteau, and J. C. Robert, "La structure professionnelle de Montréal en 1825," *RHAF* 30, no.3 (December 1976): 383—407; suggest that this middle-level group has an importance that has often been

overlooked because of the emphasis given to the well-known international merchants.

5. *Le Courrier du Canada*, April 28, 1858, gives the executive of the Institut Canadien-Français. In 1872 Pominville was a director of the New York Life Insurance Company. For the terms of the Cartier-Pominville partnership see chap. 4.

6. For a biography of Donegani see *DCB*, 9 (1976): 207–9.

7. McCord, Robert MacKay to Cartier, n.d.

8. Fees Book, Compagnie de Richelieu entries, June, October, 1851.

9. Ibid., total of all entries, 1835–53.

10. Ibid., entries for Aimé Massue, John Donegani; P. W. Shepard, "Personal History of a Young Man," PAC, MG 24, I, p.36, cited in Parks Canada file; McCord, George Hagar bill, February 8, 1849.

11. For an account of his Grand Trunk and Seminary of Montreal work, see chap. 4.

12. McCord, T. K. Ramsay, Crown Attorney, to Cartier, October 15, 1866.

13. PAC, MG 27, reel A 765, Monck Papers, Lord Carnarvon to Monck, November 24, 1866; Cartier's insistence on the propriety of his actions is in McCord, Cartier to Monck, October 17, 1866.

14. Montreal *Gazette*, March 29, 31, 1855.

15. *La Minerve*, March 9, 1855.

16. DCP, Robert Henderson to Cartier, March 31, 1871.

17. The Canadian example is best described in P.A. Linteau and J.C. Robert, "Propriété foncière et société à Montréal: une hypothèse," *RHAF* 28, no.1 (June 1974): 45–65. The proclivity of the French bourgeoisie for real-estate investment is shown in Adeline Daumard, *La bourgeoisie parisienne de 1815 à 1848* (Paris: Ecole pratique des hautes études, 1963), p.486, and Louis Bergeron, *Les capitalistes en France*, 1780–1914 (Paris: Gallimard, 1978), pp.17–36.

18. McCord, assessment notices to Cartier, 1852; bill from D. Laurent, August 24, 1853. The concentration of professional, commercial, and clerical groups in the centre of Montreal has been noted by Bernard, Linteau, and Robert, "La structure professionnelle de Montréal," p.405, and has been exhibited quantitatively in Marcel Bellavance's, "Les structures de l'espace urbain montréalais à l'époque de la Confédération," paper delivered at meeting of Learned Societies, Montreal, May 29, 1980. For a French comparison, see Louis Bergeron, *Banquiers, négociants et manufacturiers parisiens du Directoire à l'Empire* (Paris: Mouton, 1978), chap. 1.

19. *Discours*, pp.31–32; *La Minerve*, March 23, 1857.

20. McCord, statement to justice of the peace, March 24, 1848; DCP, unnotarized contract between Sylvestre Cartier and Damien Cartier, n.d.; Donation rémunérative par Jacques Cartier et son épouse à George-Etienne Cartier, leur fils, February 24, 1841. Although the 1,200 acres in the Township of Ham, Wolfe County, were held in freehold tenure, Cartier's parents took

possession of the land by the practice of *viager*, agreeing to lodge the former proprietor until his death.

21. DCP, vente par François Perrin to Cartier, June 13, 1842; devise d'une bâti se pour G. Cartier, 1843.

22. Ibid., Office of Ordnance, March 20, 1846, July 28, 1848; unpublished report of Marthe Lacombe for Parks Canada, Quebec City, p.28.

23. DCP, contracts with Joseph Laramée, and Laberge and Bertrand, January 8, 1864.

24. Ibid.,——to Cartier, March 7, 1873; Office of Ordnance to Cartier, March 20, 1846.

25. Ibid., lease by Michel Raymond from Cartier, October 10, 1870; lease by Henry Gray from Cartier, September 14, 1872.

26. Ibid., report of E. Darche, January 18, 1874.

27. Linteau and Robert, "Propriété foncière et société à Montréal," p.59; Adeline Daumard, *Les fortunes françaises au XIX siècle* (Paris: Mouton, 1973), p.153.

28. Quoted in Bergeron, *Les capitalistes en France*, p.36.

29. DCP, Maurice Cuvillier to Cartier.

30. Ibid., Sir G.-E. Cartier in account with Cuvillier and Co., 1865, 1870–73.

31. PAC, Papers of Joseph-Amable Berthelot, no.19, Cartier to Berthelot, August 25, 1841.

32. DCP, titre nouvel, February 23, 1843 (Menard, notary).

33. Ibid., Obligation Dame Marguerite Paradis et George-Etienne Cartier, June 12, 1847, (P. Chagnon, notary); promissory notes, Marguerite Paradis to Cartier, December 30, 1845, March 3, October 3, 1846, January 9, 1847.

34. McCord, Antoine-Côme Cartier to Cartier, March 13, 1854.

35. Ibid., Sylvestre Cartier to Cartier, January 22, 1849.

36. DCP, statement of Damien and George Cartier, December 28, 1840.

37. McCord, Hotel du Canada bill addressed to G.-E. Cartier, n.d.; Robert Mackay, *Montreal Directory*, 1854–55; DCP, Antoine-Côme Cartier to Cartier, July 30, 1860.

38. Lactance Papineau to L. J. Papineau, May 1845, quoted in Lionel Groulx, "Fils de grand homme," *RHAF* 10, no.1 (June 1956): 325.

39. The Fabre family are treated extensively by Gérard Parizeau, *La chronique des Fabres* (Montreal: Fides, 1978) and in various works by Jean-Louis Roy. In particular, see the latter's thesis, "Edouard-Raymond Fabre: Bourgeois Patriote du Bas-Canada, 1799–1854" (Ph.D. thesis, McGill University, 1971). Details of the Fabre estate are given in the inventory appended to this thesis. Fabre had investments in the Grand Trunk Railway (£73), the Montreal and New York Printing Telegraph Company (£25), and the Industry and Rawdon Railway (£50). See also J. L. Roy, "Livres et société bas-canadienne: croissance et expansion de la librairie Fabre, 1816–55," *Social History* 5, no.10 (November 1972):129, J.L. Roy, *Edouard-Raymond Fabre: libraire et pat-*

riote canadien (Montreal: HMH, 1974),p.24, and Montreal *Gazette*, March 24, 1855.

40. Fees Book, p.53; DCP, Lettres de bénéfices et inventaire accordés aux héritiers de feu Jacques Cartier. . ., September 20, 1841; inventory of Fabre estate, Roy, "Edouard-Raymond Fabre," p.746.

41. ANQ, E. R. Fabre papers, E. R. Fabre to Julie Bossange, June 12, 1846, quoted in Louis Richer file, Parks Canada.

42. DCP, contrat de mariage, June 9, 1846 (Girouard, notary); inventory of Fabre estate, Roy, "Edouard-Raymond Fabre."

43. ASSM, tiroir 6, file 58, photocopy of marriage certificate, June 16, 1846.

44. Adolphe-Basile Routhier, *Sir George-Etienne Cartier* (Montreal: Laval University, 1912), p.13. A prominent Conservative, judge, ultramontane, and family friend, Routhier often entertained Lady Cartier at his home on the lower St. Lawrence River.

45. Parizeau, *La chronique des Fabres*, p.128.

46. Routhier, *Sir George-Etienne Cartier*, p.13.

47. Francis Monck, *My Canadian Leaves* (London 1891), p.28.

48. PAC, MG 24, B158, Berthelot Papers, Cartier to J. A. Berthelot, August 25, 1841; L. L. La Fontaine to J. A. Berthelot, September 14, 1850; Monck, *My Canadian Leaves*, p.113.

49. Boyd, p.371; Monck, *My Canadian Leaves*, p.34.

50. Material concerning Cartier's house is largely drawn from Marthe Lacombe's report for Parks Canada.

51. McCord, Beard's Hotel bill, 1850, Sword's Hotel bill, July, 1853; information on Cartier's Quebec City residence is contained in the Parks Canada file (Quebec City) entitled "Saint Louis residence"; DCP, rent payment notice from Georgina Ruffenstein, 1868; Maria Street was renamed Laurier Street and the Colonel By Hotel now stands on the site of Cartier's house.

52. Monck, *My Canadian Leaves*, p.149; the governor general's sister-in-law described Cartier's hobby as "Love." Ibid.

53. Parks Canada (Quebec City), file of Louis Richer, E. Rodier to Cartier, n.d.; Berthelot Papers, Cartier to Berthelot, September 22, 1838.

54. McCord, Cartier to Lord Carnarvon, October 16, 1858; Cartier to Clara Pusey, October 23, 1858, January 10, 1861.

55. Parizeau, *La chronique des Fabres*, p.211.

56. DCP, baptismal certificate of Reine-Victoria Cartier, June 7, 1853; F. Pominville to Cartier, June 9, 1864; *La Minerve*, October 22, 1864.

57. Hortense Cartier diary, January 29, 1871; DCP, Pominville to Cartier, July 18, 1864, January 4, 1872; Joseph Hickson to Cartier, July 1, 1872.

58. DCP, copy of death certificate of Reine-Victoria Cartier, July 10, 1854; *La Minerve*, July 11, 1854.

59. ANQ, Chapais Collection, E. Hartigan to Cartier, December 6, 1865; Josephine Cartier diary, January 1, 1871.

60. Parizeau, *La chronique des Fabres*, p.223; Josephine Cartier diary, January 10, 1870; Hortense Cartier diary, January 1, 1871.

61, Ibid., December 25, 1872; Macdonald Papers, MG 26, no.70, vol. 200–203, no. 85862–63, Cartier to Macdonald, March 6, 1869. For other references to his desire for a son, see Best, p.102, and L. O. David, *Souvenirs et biographies* (Montreal: Beauchemin, 1911), p.161.

62. Hortense Cartier diary, December 25, 1872.

63. Ibid.

64. Ibid., July 5, 1872; "le parfait gentilhomme" referred to by Lady Cartier was the Comte d'Argence.

65. Joseph Cartier, the brother of Cartier's grandfather, married Marie-Aimée Cuvillier. For Cuvillier as landlord, see Linteau and Robert, "Propriété foncière et société à Montréal," p.60; Syme's career is described in *DCB*, 9 (1976):772–74; Gerald Tulchinsky, *Montreal Businessmen and the Growth of Industry and Transportation, 1837–55* (Toronto: University of Toronto Press, 1977), p.178.

66. *La Minerve*, October 18, 1865; ANQ, Chapais Collection, H.Langevin to wife, November 30, 1866.

67. DCP, Maurice Cuvillier to Cartier, July 29, 1865, Luce Cuvillier to Cartier, October 20, 1870.

68. Ibid., Inventaire des biens de la succession de feu l'hon. Sir George-Etienne Cartier, August 28, 1873; F. Pominville to Cartier, May 20, 1864; Maurice Cuvillier to Cartier, May 5, July 29, 1865; Cartier's will is published in *Le rapport de l'archiviste de la Province de Québec*, 1963.

69. DCP, bills from Alexander Bassano, February 12, 1869; Robert Drake, furrier, November 17, 1868; Maurice Cuvillier to Cartier, September 10, 1867; John Carroll to Cartier, May 29, 1871.

70. Parizeau, *La chronique des Fabres*, p.240; Sweeny, p.321.

71. Marthe Lacombe report for Parks Canada (Quebec City), p.50, Lady Cartier (Paris) to estate executors, August 8, 1873; DCP, Accountables of Sundries sold by auction, September, 1873. In fact, her mother, Madame Fabre, saw to it that the definition of "personal belongings" included the silver, ten chandeliers, and revenue from the sale of the family piano.

72. Hortense Cartier diary, August 25, 1871; Sweeny, p.171; DCP, Inventory of sale of George-Etienne Cartier library, January 25, 1875.

73. DCP, clipping from Toronto *Globe*, August 7, 1862; Clara Symes did become a prominent Catholic philanthropist in Montreal, married a French aristocrat, le duc de Bassano, and moved to France in 1872.

74. Ibid., Maurice Cuvillier to Cartier, September 10, 1867.

75. Daumard, *La bourgoisie parisienne*, p.138; Roland Barthes describes piano-playing and water-colour painting as the two "fausses occupations d'une jeune fille bourgeoise au XIXe siècle." *Roland Barthes par Roland Barthes* (Paris: Seuil, 1975), p.56.

76. McCord, bills from P. Gauthier, June 1853, Alex Levy, December 31, 1853; Boyd, p.326.

77. DCP, Inventaire des biens. . ., August 28, 1873.

78. Ibid., Inventory of sale of George-Etienne Cartier library, January 25, 1875.

79. J. I. Cooper, "The Political Ideas of George-Etienne Cartier," *Report*, Canadian Historical Association (1938), p.286.

80. Daumard, *La bourgeoisie parisienne*, p.354; DCP, Dawson Bros. Booksellers, June 20, 1869.

81. DCP, Inventaire des biens. . ., August 28, 1873, p.100.

82. The inventory includes six novels by the English writer Laurence Sterne but implies that they are French editions.

83. Although the 1869 purchase price is not known, the farm sold for $20,000 in 1874. DCP, Etat démontrant les recettes et les dépenses de la succession . . . Cartier, July 1885.

84. DCP, bill from George Gallagher, June 1, 1870; inventory of Limoilou estate, August 30, 1873.

85. Ibid., bill from P. Buckley for driver and cab, November 28, 1867; account with Cuvillier and Co., 1870−73; bill from Mrs. Campbell, July 9, 1866; bill from P. H. Hill, December 23, 1867; Grand Hotel bill, Paris, December 31, 1868; farm labourers were paid 90 cents a day and the groundskeeper $24 a month.

86. Ibid., receipts from Thomas Vincent, December 11, 1868, March 1, 1869, Bank of Montreal cheques to Vincent, March 4, April 1, 2, 9, September 3, 1868; handwritten inventory of Cartier's possessions, n.d.

87. Josephine Cartier diary, August 25, 1872.

88. DCP, bill from Brevoort House, New York, November 14, 1866; receipt from P. and F. Shafer, Dressing Case and Despatch Boxmakers, April 26, 1867.

89. ANQ, Chapais Collection, Box 2, H. Langevin to Edmond Langevin, January 13, 1869.

90. *La Minerve,* March 23, 1867, February 12, 1869; Cartier speech to Stadacona Club in Montreal *Gazette*, December 28, 1869.

91. ANQ, Chapais Collection, Box 25, invitation to meet Queen Victoria, March 19, 1869; *L'Opinion Publique*, n.d., quoted in *La Minerve*, May 29, 1873.

92. *La Minerve*, March 27, 1867; *L'Opinion Publique*, January 8, 1870.

93. McCord, assorted invitations to Cartier, House of Commons *Debates*, April 29, 1869; Josephine Cartier diary, January 5, 1873.

94. McCord, Hortense Cartier to D.R. McCord, June 1, 1913; DCP, assorted bills from Beard and Nash, November, December, 1866; bill from William Hawes, Spectacle Maker, December 18, 1866; receipt from Robert Douglas, haircutter, March 28, 1868, January 19, March 27, 1869; bill from H. P. Truefitt, March 17, 1869.

95. R. Rumilly, *Histoire de la Société Saint Jean-Baptiste* (Montreal: L'Aurore, 1975), p.56; J. Léopold Gagner, *Duvernay et la Société Saint Jean-Baptiste*, (Montreal: Chantecler, 1952), p.40; Monck, *My Canadian Leaves*, January 11, 1865, p.113.

96. ANQ, Chapais Collection, Box 8, Cartier to Lord Monck, July 2, 1867.

97. DCP, handwritten note, "the arms of Sir George Cartier are. . .," n.d.; Cartier's motto was *Franc et Sans Dol* (Frank and Without Deceit).

98. Sweeny, p.25; McCord, militia appointment, July 14, 1847; *La Minerve*, May 12, 13, 24, 1862; *Discours*, March 31, 1868, p.566. Regiments which did not obtain full contingents by voluntary means were entitled to use conscription (*tirage au sort*) to fill their ranks. Military service was obligatory in time of war, although it was possible to hire a replacement.

99. Cartier is quoted in Montreal *Gazette*, December 28, 1869; House of Commons *Debates*, March 31, May 1, 1868; *Discours*, March 31, 1868, p.566.

100. A good description of Montesquieu's anglophilism can be found in Raymond Aron, *Les étapes de la pensée sociologique* (Paris: Gallimard, 1967), p.42; André Siegfried, *Mes souvenirs de la IIIe République: mon père et son temps, Jules Siegfried, 1836–1922* (Paris: Editions du Grand Siècle, 1946); Yvan Lamonde, *Les bibliothèques de collectivités à Montréal* (Montreal: Bibliothèque nationale du Québec, 1979), p.31.

101. Barthes, *Roland Barthes par Roland Barthes*, p.56.

102. *Madame Bovary*, pt.III, chap. vi.

103. See, for example, the photograph of Cartier, Luce Cuvillier's brother, and three priests (p.40).

Notes to Chapter Three

1. ANQ, Duvernay Papers, no.471, F. Amiot to Duvernay, February 3, 1841.

2. DCP, Chevalier de Lorimier to Cartier, February 12, 1839.

3. *Rapport de l'archiviste de la province de Québec*, 1925–26, Cartier to Charles Buller, September 20, 1838; PAC, Berthelot Papers, Cartier to J. A. Berthelot, September 22, 1838.

4. L. O. David, *Biographies et portraits* (Montreal: Beauchemin et Valois, 1876), p.151.

5. Cartier speech in legislative assembly, *La Minerve*, June 10, 1850, cited in Best, p.109.

6. Cartier speech in St. Denis, September 1844, cited in Boyd, p.65.

7. Jacques Monet, *The Last Cannon Shot* (Toronto: University of Toronto Press, 1969), p.45.

8. George Brown was harsh in his judgement of La Fontaine's evolution: "He climbed the ladder a liberal, the friend of the people, the friend of progress, the enemy of priestcraft and he kicked it away when he got to the top—became extremely conservative, afraid of popular influence, a devout son of mother church and a baptizer of bells." PAC, Brown Papers, no.867, Brown to Anne Brown, March 2, 1864.

9. ANQ, Duvernay Papers, Louis Perrault to Duvernay, September 22, 1840.

10. Cartier to La Fontaine, September 18, 1842, cited in Boyd, p.87; *Discours*, pp.1–3.

11. *Discours*, p.9; Aimé Massue, the seigneur of Varennes, was one of Cartier's chief legal clients in the 1840s.

12. Donald Creighton, *John A. Macdonald: The Young Politician* (Toronto: Macmillan, 1952), p.340; Lena Newman, *The John A. Macdonald Album* (Montreal: Tundra Books, 1974), p.89.

13. Monet, *The Last Cannon Shot*, p.322; PAC, Sydney Bellingham Memoirs, p.202; PAC, Macdonald Papers, no.85813, Cartier to Macdonald, September 1, 1866; Boyd, p.361.

14. *Le Nouveau Monde*, quoted in *La Minerve*, May 21, 1873; W. Notman and Fennings Taylor, *Portraits of British America* (Montreal: W. Notman, 1865−68), 1:122. George Brown did give Cartier top marks for stamina: "Would you believe it? Cartier commenced on Thursday at four o'clock and spoke till 6: he resumed at half past eight and spoke till a quarter past eleven: resumed yesterday at three and spoke till six: resumed at half past seven and spoke till a quarter to one!!! The little wretch screetched—is that the way to spell it?—thirteen hours in one speech! They used to charge me with being long-winded but Cartier outdoes all the _____ past, present or to come." Brown Papers, no. 865, Brown to wife, March 1, 1865. This hostility to Cartier in their private correspondance contrasts sharply with the public rhetoric of the fathers of Confederation. Joseph Howe was another who skewered Cartier privately: "Cartier is the most overrated man in the House. He screams like a seagull in a gale wind, has a . . . dictatorial manner and an illogical mind." Joseph Howe to wife, November 22, 1867, quoted in Best, p.446.

15. PAC, J. A. Berthelot Papers, La Fontaine to Berthelot, July 30, 1850; Best, p.136, states that Cartier and Morin were related by marriage. Detailed accounts of the political events of the 1850s and 1860s and Cartier's role therein are included in J.M.S. Careless, *The Union of the Canadas: The Growth of Canadian Institutions*, 1841−57 (Toronto: McClelland and Stewart, 1967) and his *Brown of the Globe*, 2 vols. (Toronto: Macmillan, 1959, 1963); Paul Cornell, *The Alignment of Political Groups in Canada*, 1841−67 (Toronto: University of Toronto Press, 1962); and Jean-Paul Bernard, *Les Rouges: Libéralisme, nationalisme et anticléricalisme au milieu du XIXe siècle* (Montreal: Les presses de l'université du Québec, 1971).

16. *Discours*, p.31; McCord, A. N. Morin to Cartier, November 6, 1851, Cartier to Morin, November 7, 1851.

17. *La Minerve*, July 15, 1854.

18. Ibid., September 7, 9, 1854; the office of provincial secretary reflected the dualism of the Canadian administrative structure since separate bureaucracies were maintained for the two sections of Canada. J. E. Hodgetts, *Pioneer Public Service: An Administrative History of the United Canadas* (Toronto: University of Toronto Press, 1955).

19. *Census of Canada*, 1870−71, 5:33; Rumilly, *Histoire de la province de Québec*, (Montreal: Fides, 1940), 1:73.

20. *La Minerve*, April 22, 1872.

21. *Census of Canada*, 1870−71, 5:33. This may be compared with Toronto's density of 6,025 people a square mile in 1871 and 5,172 in Quebec City.

22. The census of 1871 recorded 9,019 people over the age of twenty unable to write. *Census of Canada, 1870−71*, 2:207.

23. Ibid., 2:302; more extensive examples of conditions can be found in Bettina Bradbury, "The Family Economy and Work in an Industrializing City: Montreal in the 1870's," *Historical Papers*, Canadian Historical Association (1979), p.75.

24. See chap. 4.

25. *La Minerve*, April 13, 1843, cited in Best, p.63.

26. Francis Monck, *My Canadian Leaves* (London, 1891), p.149.

27. Alan Dever, "Economic Development and the Lower-Canadian Assembly, 1828−40" (M.A. thesis, McGill University, 1976), develops this theme convincingly for the pre-rebellion period.

28. *La Minerve*, November 2, 1852; for treatment of the Grand Trunk, see chap. 4.

29. *Discours*, March 6, 1860; House of Commons *Debates*, December 3, 1867.

30. *Discours*, March 20, 1850.

31. Ibid., October 27, 1854.

32. Ibid., March 16, 1860; before passage of this bill, mortgage-holders had little protection from the clandestine sale of the land on which they held the mortgage.

33. Ibid., p. 221.

34. House of Commons Debates, March 27, 1867.

35. He also supported the Montreal Colonization Railway in public, but since it competed with the Grand Trunk Railway, did his best to sabotage it privately.

36. Montreal *Gazette*, September 5, 1867.

37. *Royal Commission on the Canadian Pacific Railway* (Ottawa: 1873), testimony of J. J. C. Abbott, p.174.

38. *La Minerve*, April 14, 1853; for a biography of John Young, see *DCB*, 10 (1972):722−28.

39. For Quebec City's fears, see Fernand Ouellet, *Histoire de la Chambre de Commerce de Québec* (Quebec: Les presses de l'université Laval, 1959).

40. See chap. 4.

41. *Discours*, p.63.

42. Ibid., August 7, 1870, p.692.

43. McCord, St. Jean Baptiste Society receipts, 1846−48.

44. Ibid., Minutes, meeting of Montreal Bar Association, March 21, 1857; J. H. L. Beaudry to Cartier, April 17, 1857.

45. Ibid., membership ticket, Repeal Association of Ireland, 1844−45.

46. *La Minerve*, January 17, 1854; McCord, receipt for £25 contribution to relief fund, July 8, 1852.

47. *La Minerve*, June 27, 1854.

48. Monet, *The Last Cannon Shot*, p.277.

49. Best, p.107; *Discours*, March 27, 1860, p.233. Dorion charged that the

division of Montreal into three separate constituencies was gerrymandering on Cartier's part against the city's Irish and francophone voters. ANQ, Chapais Collection, Box 8, Cartier to Langevin, July 11, 1867.

50. Best, p.143; Soeur de Saint-Joseph de Saint-Hyacinthe, *La petite histoire de chez nous* (St. Hyacinthe: Historical Society of St. Hyacinthe, 1938), 38:91; Bernard, *Les Rouges*, p.234.

51. *La Minerve*, August 27, 1853; McCord, receipt from Lower Canada Agricultural Society, 1849–50.

52. McCord, Bishop of St. Hyacinthe to Cartier, March 24, 1863.

53. ANQ, Labelle Papers, Cartier to Antoine Labelle, February 5, 1863; Archives du Séminaire de Québec, Cartier to Mgr. Marquis, April 24, 1867.

54. Montreal *Gazette*, April 25, 1844. Francis Hincks was involved in a fracas on Notre Dame Street in which an Irishman was compelled to "swallow one of his own teeth." *Pilot*, April 16, 1844; according to the *Gazette*, April 13, 1844, French Canadians played little part in the riots because of their "natural aversion" to fighting.

55. Montreal *Gazette*, April 25, 1844; Francis Hincks, *Reminiscences of His Public Life* (Montreal: Drysdale and Co., 1884), p.130. The role of the military in mid-nineteenth century is described in Elinor Kyte Senior, *British Regulars in Montreal: An Imperial Garrison, 1832–1854* (Montreal: McGill-Queen's University Press, 1981); the author graciously gave me access to her research notes on the election of 1844.

56. Montreal *Gazette*, April 23, 1844.

57. Ibid., April 25, 1844; *Pilot*, April 26, 1844.

58. *La Minerve*, September 8, 1854.

59. *Le Pays*, January 16, 1858.

60. PAC, Cartier Papers, M. Lanctot to Cartier, September 17, 1872; *L'Union Nationale*, September 12, 1867; T. P. Slattery, *The Assassination of D'Arcy McGee* (Toronto: Doubleday, 1968), p.87, quotes Cartier on the availability of Irish votes.

61. Normand Séquin, "L'Opposition canadienne-française aux élections de 1867 dans la grande région de Montréal" (M.A. thesis, University of Ottawa, 1968), pp.111–12.

62. Cartier to P. J. O. Chauveau, October 22, 1867, cited in Best, p.439.

63. *Le Nouveau Monde*, August 27, 1872; Rumilly, *Histoire de la province de Québec*, 1:219; *Le National*, August 29, 1872.

64. During the campaign of September 1867 the Montreal *Gazette* described Médéric Lanctôt as a communist. Thomas White, editor of the *Gazette*, told the *Royal Commission on the Pacific Railway* (Ottawa: 1873), p.186, how his paper was helped by Hugh Allan. *Les Mélanges religieux* was edited by Hector Langevin, Cartier's law student and future lieutenant. Under Langevin's direction the paper vigorously supported the Reform cause, berating the annexationists and dismissing Papineau as "cracked." Andrée Désilets, *Hector-Louis Langevin: un père de la Confédération canadienne, 1826-1906* (Quebec: Les presses de l'université Laval, 1969), p.45.

65. McCord, bills from *La Minerve*, 1849, and the *Pilot*, July 30, 1846.
66. L. A. Dessaulles quoted in *Le Pays*, November 18, 1858.
67. *Le Pays*, March 13, 1858.
68. PAC, Ministère des affaires étrangères à Paris, correspondance commerciale et politique des consuls français à Québec, 1856−73, January 21, 1860, cited in Louis Richer file, Parks Canada (Quebec City).
69. Archives du Séminaire de Québec, Curé Labelle to Langevin, July 30, 1870.
70. Montreal *Gazette*, May 4, 1855; ANQ, Chapais Collection, Box 8, Cartier to Langevin, August 31, 1858; *Le Pays*, November 25, 1858.
71. *Le Pays*, January 19, 1858.
72. Montreal *Gazette*, May 20, 1862.
73. House of Commons *Debates*, March 30, 1868.
74. L. H. Masson in House of Commons *Debates*, March 30, 1868.
75. Ibid.
76. ANQ, Chapais Collection, Box 10, Luc Desilets to Cartier, October 2, 1868.
77. House of Commons *Debates*, May 1, 12, 1868.
78. See Fernand Dumont, "Idéologie et conscience historique dans la société canadienne-française du XIXe siècle," in J. P. Bernard, ed., *Les idéologies québécoises au XIXe siècle* (Montreal: Boréal Express, 1973), p.75−76.
79. *La Minerve*, March 24, 1859.
80. McCord, D. M. Armstrong to Cartier, May 4, 1857.
81. A report on this growing collaboration can be seen in Luther Holton's letter to George Brown, October 14, 1859, PAC, Brown Papers, no. 447.
82. See the program published in Rumilly, *Histoire de la province de Québec*, 1:200. In the standard work on the Rouges, *Les Rouges: libéralisme, nationalisme et anticléricalisme au milieu du XIXe siècle*, Jean-Paul Bernard gives more emphasis to Rouge liberalism and less to the consensus with conservatives on economic development.
83. ANQ, Duvernay Papers, Cartier to Duvernay, January 10, 1840.
84. Cartier to La Fontaine, September 18, 1842, cited in Boyd, p.87.
85. ANQ, Chapais Collection, Box 25, Guillaume Lévesque to Cartier, June 19, 1844; Best, app. 14, p.640.
86. Monet, *The Last Cannon Shot*, p.323; Best, p.649; Bernard, *Les Rouges*, p.41; Chapais Collection, Box 25, Joseph Doutre to Cartier, August 4, 8, 1848.
87. *La Minerve*, February 23, 25, March 2, 1854.
88. Boyd, p.351.
89. *Discours*, speech at Ludger Duvernay funeral, October 21, 1855, p.66.
90. Ibid., July 13, 1866, p.495.
91. Best, p.666; *La Minerve*, March 18, 1853.
92. Ibid., April 16, 1861; *Discours*, p.150; J. I. Cooper, "The Political Ideas of George-Etienne Cartier," *Report*, Canadian Historical Association (1942), p.286, concluded that Cartier was a man of "political action, but very little political theory." However, there is a strong resemblance in both tone and

content between Cartier's rhetoric and the writings of conservative theorists like Burke, who insisted that "the road to eminence and power . . . ought not be made too easy" and "the characteristic essence of property, formed out of the combined principles of its acquisition and conservation, is to be unequal." Quoted in Michael Curtis, ed., *The Great Political Theories* (New York: Avon, 1961), pp.52−53.

93. *Discours*, November 7, 1854; House of Commons *Debates*, November 19, 1867.

94. *La Minerve*, April 16, 1856.

95. In 1867 Cartier also sat on the provincial assembly's committee on election privileges and on the public accounts committee. *Journals of the Legislative Assembly of Quebec*, 1867, p.7; for further examples of the subordination of Quebec to the federal government, see the author's article "Federalism in Quebec" in Bruce Hodgins, ed., *Federalism in Canada and Australia* (Waterloo: Wilfrid Laurier University Press, 1978), pp.97−108.

96. *La Minerve*, June 14, 1853.

97. Best, p.118; Cartier's own employees were paid 90 cents a day.

98. *Discours*, July 13, 1866, p.495.

99. Ibid., p.425.

100. Monet, *The Last Cannon Shot*, p.356.

101. *La Minerve*, October 15, 1849, quoted in Best, app. 19, p.664.

102. *La Minerve*, April 19, 1856.

103. David Knight, *Choosing Canada's Capital* (Toronto: McClelland and Stewart, 1977), pp.14, 110−15.

104. *Journals of the Legislative Assembly of Canada*, April 10, 1856, p.281.

105. *La Minerve*, April 9, 1856.

106. Governor General Head, memorandum, n.d., quoted in Knight, *Choosing Canada's Capital*, p.166; *Discours*, February 2, 1859, pp.173−74.

107. Knight, *Choosing Canada's Capital*, p.115; O. D. Skelton, *The Life and Times of Sir Alexander Tilloch Galt* (Toronto: Oxford University Press, 1920), p.202.

108. Knight, *Choosing Canada's Capital*, p.182.

109. Ibid., p.x.

110. W. L. Morton, *The Critical Years: The Union of British North America, 1857-73* (Toronto: McClelland and Stewart, 1964), p.65.

111. P. B. Waite, *John A. Macdonald: His Life and World* (Toronto: McGraw-Hill, Ryerson, 1975), p.62.

112. Skelton, *Sir Alexander Tilloch Galt*, p.96.

113. PAC, Brown Papers, no.953, Brown to wife, June 20, 1864.

114. Ibid., October 27, 1864.

115. *La Minerve*, July 16, 1864, quoted in J. C. Bonenfant, *French Canadians and the Birth of Confederation* (Ottawa: Canadian Historical Association, 1966), p.14.

116. Cartier in Legislative Assembly, February 7, 1865, quoted in P. B. Waite, ed., *The Confederation Debates in the Province of Canada, 1865* (Toronto: McClelland and Stewart, 1963).

117. In the final conference in London in the spring of 1867 Cartier apparently did block Macdonald's attempts to increase centralization. See J. C. Bonenfant, *La naissance de la Confédération* (Montreal: Leméac, 1969), p.107.

118. Waite, *Confederation Debates*, p.115.

119. Cartier in Legislative Assembly, February 7, 1865, Waite, *Confederation Debates,* pp.50–51.

120. Ibid., p.50.

121. McCord, clipping from *Canadian News*, April 27, 1865.

122. Waite, *Confederation Debates*, pp.88, 95.

123. Ibid., pp.88, 148–49.

124. H.G. Joly speech in Legislative Assembly, February 7, 1865, ibid., p.96.

125. Cartier in Legislative Assembly, February 7, 1865, ibid., p.51.

126. *La Minerve*, n.d., quoted in Bonenfant, *French Canadians and the Birth of Confederation*, p.14.

127. See chap. 4.

128. Quoted in Bonenfant, *French Canadians and the Birth of Confederation*, p.15; see also Cartier speech in Waite, *Confederation Debates*, p.52, and Walter Ullmann, "The Quebec Bishops and Confederation," in Ramsay Cook, ed., *Confederation* (Toronto: University of Toronto Press, 1967), pp.48–69.

129. Vicar General Truteau to Vicar General Cazeau, February 20, 1865, quoted in Ullmann, "The Quebec Bishops," p.56.

130. *La Minerve*, May 30, 1866, cited in Ullmann, "The Quebec Bishops," p.57.

131. Quebec *Morning Chronicle*, February 23, 1865.

132. John Rose quoted in Quebec *Morning Chronicle*, February 23, 1865.

133. McCord, Cartier to John Rose, February 21, 1867.

134. Quebec *Morning Chronicle*, March 11, 1865.

135. Ibid., March 20, August 10, 1865.

136. ANQ, Chapais Collection, Box 8, Cartier to Langevin, April 17, 1866; Langevin to Cartier, April 19, 1866.

137. Boyd, p.399.

138. A full description of the campaign of 1867 is contained in Gaetan Gervais, "Médéric Lanctôt et *L'Union Nationale*" (M.A. thesis, University of Ottawa, 1968).

139. *L'Union Nationale*, March 20, 1867.

140. Ibid., March 30, 1867.

141. For the politics of this newspaper, see Gérard Bouchard, "Apogée et déclin de l'idéologie ultramontaine à travers le journal *Le Nouveau Monde, 1867–1900*," *Recherches Sociographiques* 10, nos.2–3 (1969):261–91.

142. Norman Séguin, "L'Opposition canadienne-française aux élections de 1867 dans la grande région de Montréal" (M.A. thesis, University of Ottawa, 1968), p.119.

Notes to Chapter Four

1. Minutes, St. Jean Baptiste Society, vol. 1 (1843–81), p.4.
2. Rumilly, *Histoire de la Société Saint-Jean Baptiste* (Montreal: L'Aurore, 1975), p.56; J. Léopold Gagner, *Duvernay et la Société Saint-Jean Baptiste* (Montreal: Chantecler, 1952), p.40.
3. Minutes, St. Jean Baptiste Society, vol. 1 (1843–81), pp.84, 135, 195.
4. Keith D. Hunte, "The Development of the System of Education in Canada East, 1841–67: An Historical Survey" (M.A. thesis, McGill University, 1962), p.171; André Jabarrère-Paulé, *Les instituteurs laïques au Canada-français 1836-1900* (Quebec: Les presses de l'université Laval, 1956), p.18.
5. *Discours*, April 15, 1856, p.103; clerical attitudes to education before 1837 are examined fully in Richard Chabot, *Le Curé de campagne et la contestation locale au Québec de 1791 aux troubles de 1837* (Montreal: HMH, 1975) and in Fernand Ouellet, "L'enseignement primaire, responsabilité des églises ou de l'état (1801–36)," in his *Eléments d'histoire sociale du Bas-Canada* (Montreal: HMH, 1972), pp.259–80. French-Canadian hostility to the Royal Institutes is examined in Réal Boulianne, "The French Canadians and the Schools of the Royal Institution for the Advancement Of Learning, 1820–29," *Social History* 5, no.10 (November 1972):145–64. Lay teachers are treated in André Labarrère-Paulé, *Les instituteurs laïques au Canada-français, 1836-1900* (Quebec: Les presses de l'université Laval, 1965). Of particular interest because of its conclusions on the social implications of literacy is Allan Greer, "The Pattern of Literacy in Quebec, 1845–99," *Social History* 11, no.22 (November 1978):295–335. The standard work on Quebec education is Louis-Philippe Audet, *Le système scolaire de la province de Québec*, 2 vols. (Quebec: Les presses de l'université Laval, 1951).
6. Greer, "Pattern of Literacy in Quebec," p.315.
7. McCord, Antoine-Côme Cartier to G.-E. Cartier, September 29, 1854.
8. See, for example, Jacques Monet's biography of La Fontaine in *DCB*, 9 (1976):440–51.
9. *Statutes of Canada*, 9 Vic., cap. 27, June 9, 1846, "Act to ... make better provision for Elementary Education in Lower Canada."
10. Hunte, "Development of the System of Education," p.164; L. P. Audet, *Histoire du conseil de l'instruction publique* (Montreal: Leméac, 1964), p.18.
11. Hunte, "Development of the System of Education," pp.126, 161.
12. Montreal *Gazette*, December 18, 1855.
13. Thomas Chapais, "La guerre des éteignoirs," *Report*, Royal Society of Canada, ser. 3 (May 1928), pp.1–6; Audet, *Histoire du conseil de l'instruction publique*, p.8. Not enough is known about these uprisings to compare them to English or European examples of parochial reaction to centralization. However, the participation of some deputies and other members of the local élite in the unrest is interesting in the light of E. P. Thompson's argument that some English uprisings occurred "under the licence of a part of the local Establishment." *The Making of the English Working Class*, p.80; see

also E. B. Hobsbawn, "Les soulèvements de la campagne anglaise, 1798–1850," *Annales* 23 (January-February 1968):9–30.

14. PAC, MG24, B158, Joseph-Amable Berthelot Papers, pp.209–11, La Fontaine to Berthelot, July 30, 1850.

15. Chapais, "La guerre des éteignoirs," p.4.

16. DCP, Joseph Guigues, Bishop of Bytown to Cartier, December 16, 1856.

17. Audet, *Histoire du conseil de l'instruction publique*, p.26.

18. *Discours*, April 7, 18, 1856, pp.87, 105.

19. *Statutes of Canada*, 19 Vic., cap.54, June 19, 1856, "An Act ... for promotion of superior education ..."

20. Pensions for "worn out" teachers were also instituted. *Statutes of Canada*, 19 Vic., cap.14, May 16, 1856.

21. Montreal *Gazette*, April 3, 1856.

22. ASSM, tiroir 46, no.53, Constitution et règlements de l'association des instituteurs.

23. *Le Journal de l'instruction* 3, no.3 (March 1859).

24. *Discours*, April 7, 1856, p.97; Audet, *Histoire du conseil de l'instruction publique*, p.37.

25. Cartier reported to the assembly that the number of schools in Quebec had increased from 2,352 to over 3,000 in the two-year period, 1853–55. *Discours*, February 20, 1856, p.70. Greer describes this growth in literacy and speculates on possible repercussions on the birth rate, the commercialization of agriculture, and the development of an industrial work force. "Pattern of Literacy in Quebec," pp. 334–35.

26. The Quebec pattern corresponds to Jean-Pierre Rioux's model, according to which the goals of mid-nineteenth century educators, whether Prussian, Anglo-Saxon, or French, were the same: "permettre aux futurs citoyens d'accomplir leur devoir civique et militaire, prêcher la resignation à la main d'oeuvre agricole ou industrielle." *La révolution industrielle, 1780-1880* (Paris: Seuil, 1971), p.206.

27. DCP, Bishop Joseph Guigues to Cartier, December 16, 1856.

28. *Discours*, Cartier speeches, April 1, 15, 1856, pp.79, 103; Arthur Turcotte in assembly, Montreal *Gazette*, April 21, 1855.

29. Audet, *Histoire du conseil de l'instruction publique*, p.37.

30. Orrin B. Rexford, "Teacher Training in the Province of Quebec: A Historical Study to 1857" (M.A. thesis, McGill University, 1936), p.89.

31. Montreal *Gazette*, February 9, 1856.

32. Rexford, "Teacher Training," p.82.

33. *Discours*, April 1, 1856, p.79; see also the *Gazette's* report of the same speech, April 3, 1856, which cited Cartier's somewhat contradictory statement that "two languages would be taught in all schools" and *La Minerve's* assertion (April 16, 1856) that Cartier had stated that English would be taught in all three normal schools.

34. Quoted in John Brierley, "Quebec's Civil Law Codification," *McGill Law Journal* 144 (1968): 530. His account stresses the technical need for

codification. On the other hand, Yves Zoltvany, "Esquisse de la Coutume de Paris," *RHAF* 25, no.3 (December 1971): 367, emphasizes that the Custom of Paris confined the Quebec bourgeoisie "dans une structure essentiellement non-capitaliste." This general theme is extended by Michael E. Tigar and Madeleine R. Levy, *Law and the Rise of Capitalism* (New York: Monthly Review, 1977). André Morel emphasizes the lack of public debate on the proposed codification, aside from sections dealing with marriage. He finds this silence particularly surprising on the part of judges and bar associations. "La codification devant l'opinion publique de l'époque," in Jacques Boucher and André Morel, *Livre du centenaire du Code civil* (Montreal: Les presses de l'université de Montréal, 1970), pp.37–38.

35. Thomas McCord, *The Civil Code of Lower Canada* (Montreal: Dawson Brothers, 1867), p.11.

36. Quebec *Morning Chronicle*, February 1, 1865.

37. Ibid.; Sweeny, p.113.

38. *Statutes of Canada*, 20 Vic., cap.43, 1857, p.182, 185.

39. Brierley, "Quebec's Civil Law Codification," p.583.

40. *Civil Code, Codifiers Report* (Quebec; 1865)

41. *Statutes of Canada*, 20 Vic., cap. 44, June 10, 1857, "An Act to Amend the Judicature Acts of Lower Canada."

42. *La Minerve*, March 14, 1857; *Statutes of Canada*, 20 Vic., cap. 45, June 10, 1857, "An Act for settling the Law concerning lands held in Free and Common Socage in Lower Canada."

43. The factor of commutations in Montreal land values, the importance of the St. Gabriel farm in orienting city road, canal, and rail development, and the social and educational role of the Sulpician seigneurs in Montreal provide ample evidence of seigneurialism as an urban force. Straightforward descriptions of seigneurialism are contained in R. C. Harris, *The Seigneurial System in Early Canada: A Geographical Study* (Madison: University of Wisconsin Press, 1967). Its implications for eighteenth-century Montreal are outlined in Louise Dechêne, *Habitants et marchands de Montréal au XVIIe siècle* (Paris: Plon, 1974).

44. For a wide-ranging debate of this transformation see Maurice Dobbs and Paul Sweezy, *Du féodalisme au capitalisme: problèmes de la transition* (Paris Maspero, 1977). The abolition of seigneurial tenure in Canada is examined in Ouellet, *Eléments d'histoire sociale du Bas-Canada* (Montreal: HMH, 1972), pp.91-112, 297-318, Ouellet, *Le Bas Canada, 1791-1840* (Ottawa: University of Ottawa Press, 1976), pp.221-46, and in J. P. Wallot, *Un Québec qui bougeait: trame socio-politique au tournant du XIXe siècle* (Montreal: Boréal Express, 1973).

45. Lewis Drummond speaking in Legislative Assembly, 1853, cited in Ouellet, *Eléments d'histoire sociale*, p.300; for a short description of the bourgeoisie's relationship to the feudal structure, see Régine Pernoud, *Les origines de la bourgeoisie* (Paris: Presses Universitaires de France, 1969); in

1831 eighty-four seigneuries were held by English speakers, Ouellet, *Eléments d'histoire sociale*, p. 100.

46. Alexander Galt, speech in London, published in Isaac Buchanan, *The Relations of the Industry of Canada with the Mother Country and the United States* (Montreal 1864), p.315.

47. The philosophical basis of Viger's defence of seigneurialism is described in Ouellet, *Eléments d'histoire sociale*, pp.305-15.

48. *Discours*, April 8, 1859, p.193; *DCB,* 9 (1976): 145, cites Cartier's description that seigneurialism "retards the progress of the country."

49. Best, p.109; *La Minerve*, May 3, 1854.

50. *Discours*, March 20, 1853, p.36.

51. Ouellet, *Le Bas Canada*, p.227; Gilles Bourque and Anne Legaré, *Le Québec: la question nationale* (Paris: Maspero, 1979), p.60, identify but without documentation "la résistance paysanne" as the main obstacle to the commercialization of agriculture on the seigneuries.

52. *Discours*, June 25, 1850, p.24. Nine years later *La Minerve*, April 12, 1859, was still accusing opponents of abolition of being "socialiste."

53. *Journals of the Legislative Assembly of Canada*, 1841-51, pp.488-90.

54. J.C. Taché, "The Seigneurial System in Canada and Plan of Commutation," in *Index to the Journals of the Assembly of Canada*, 1852-68, p.794. The Taché pamphlet, published by the Anti-Seigneurial Committee of Montreal, was translated into English and published by the government.

55. *Discours*, February 14, 1855, p.57; F. Hincks, *The Seigneurial Question: Its Present Position* (Quebec, 1854), pp.6-7.

56. They based this claim on the fact that the seminary was on the land of the Abbey of Saint-Germain and had received its original letters-patent from the abbey. Pierre Boisard, *La compagnie de Saint-Sulpice: trois siècles d'histoire*, 2 vols. (Paris: n. p., 1941). The Sulpician experience in Canada has been described in several places by Olivier Maurault, particularly in *Le Grand Séminaire de Montréal* (Montreal: Association des anciens élèves du Grand Séminaire, 1940). Henri Gauthier's *Sulpitiana* (Montreal: Bureau des oeuvres paroissiales de Saint-Jacques, 1926) is useful for statistical details.

57. Boisard, *Saint-Sulpice*, p.81; Joseph-Vincent Quiblier, "Notice sur le Séminaire de Montréal," manuscript, 1846, ASSM, tiroir 70.

58. Gérard Bouchard and André Larose, "Le réglement du contenu des actes de baptême, mariage, sépulture, au Québec des origines à nos jours," *RHAF*, 30, no.1 (June 1976): 77, show the civic role of parish records.

59. Boisard, *Saint-Sulpice*, 1:124; the offer of eighteen months' grace to return to France was made to all residents of New France.

60. Quiblier, "Notice," p.2. Two other communities—the Récollets and the Jesuits — suffering from the same recruiting restraint disappeared, leaving the Sulpicians and the Seminary of Quebec as the only male religious houses in Canada.

61. See for example, Viscount Goderich's letter to Lord Aylmer, September

13, 1831, quoted in Georges E. Baillargeon, *La survivance du régime seigneur-ial à Montréal* (Ottawa: Cercle du livre, 1968), p.231; see also the House of Lords debate, March 4, 1841, *Hansard*, vol. 56, ser. 3, p.1322.

62. Quiblier, "Notice," p.2. In their opposition to the rebellions, the Sulpi-cians were joined by Bishop Lartique, himself a Sulpician, and the majority of the clergy who were hostile to the liberal professions and suspicious of their use of nationalism. See, for example, Richard Chabot, *Le curé de campagne et la contestation locale au Québec de 1791 aux troubles de 1837-8* (Montreal: HMH, 1975), especially pp.100, 110, 213.

63. Bishop of Exeter speaking in House of Lords, March 4, 1841, *Hansard*, vol.56, p.1321; C. Buller, "Report from the Chief Secretary, on the Commuta-tion of the Feudal Tenures in the Island of Montreal, and other Seigniories in the Possession of the Seigniory of St. Sulpice of Montreal," October 31, 1838, app. E of Durham's Report, quoted in Baillargeon, *La survivance du régime seigneurial*, p.243; Quiblier, "Notice," p.8; *Statutes of Canada*, 3 Vic., cap.30, "Ordinance of 1840"; Wellington quoted in *Hansard*, March 4, 1841, p.1336.

64. ASSM, vol.180, livre de caisse, 1865-77.

65. *La Minerve*, July 12, 1847.

66. In 1871 Cartier received a $1,000 retainer from the seminary. At his death he had outstanding debts (three commutations plus interest) of $1,733 with the seminary (see table 5). Although the retainers were much smaller, the Sulpicians did hire lawyers of other political persuasions such as Louis Sicotte and the firm of Dorion, Dorion and Geoffrion. ASSM, lawyer account book, p. 191.

67. *Discours*, February 14, 1866, p. 475.

68. François Lagrave, "Les frères des écoles chrétiennes au Canada, "*Report, Société d'histoire de l'église catholique* (1969), p. 45.

69. ASSM, vol. 180, livre de caisse, 1865-73.

70. Members of the society deposited their contributions with the Sulpicians. When a member died, the seminary forwarded $8 to the parish to provide the service, coffin, and hearse.

71. *Discours*, April 8, 1859. This slow rural abolition suited the Sulpicians. Seigneurial revenues were maintained while urban commutations returned important amounts of investment capital. Conditions at the Lake of Two Mountains seigneury have been described in Christian Dessureault's paper, "Lac des Deux-Montagnes," presented at a meeting of the Institut d'histoire, Ottawa, October 19, 1979.

72. *Discours*, April 8, 1859, p. 197.

73. Ibid., April 8, 1859, p.193.

74. ASSM, Joseph Comte correspondence file, Comte to Cartier, November 9, 13, 1854, Comte to Lewis Drummond, November 20, 1854; *Statutes of Canada*, 18 Vic., cap. 3, "Seigneurial Act of 1854."

75. Archives de la Bibliothèque Nationale de Montréal, Biens du Séminaire, no. 192, Cartier to Joseph Comte, March 25, 1859, no. 191, M.D. Granet to Cartier, 1858.

76. Ibid., no.193, M.D. Granet to Comte, March 3, 1859.

77. ASSM, Cahier 1, Report of the Assembly of Eleven, March 10, 1859.

78. *La Minerve*, April 12, 20, 1850; *Discours*, April 8, 1859, pp. 193-99; *Statutes of Canada*, 22 Vic., cap. 48, "Seigneurial Act of 1859," sec. 20.

79. For an account of the Rouge-Grit split over seigneurial tenure, see Brown Papers, vol. 393, Lewis Drummond to Brown, April 30, 1859, Brown to Laberge, May 2, 1859.

80. Cartier's own example is interesting. After his death his executors paid the seminary $1,149 for the commutation of three of his properties plus $586 in accumulated interest charges. DCP, Report of executors of estate of G.E. Cartier, 1888, p. 10.

81. Galt speech, January 1, 1860, quoted in Isaac Buchanan, *The Relations of the Industry of Canada with the Mother Country and the United States* (Montreal, 1864), p. 315.

82. ASSM, vol. 180, livre de caisse, 1865−73; vol. 251, cahier des créanciers, 1871−1921.

83. *Le Courrier du Canada*, July 30, 1860.

84. ANQ, Labelle Papers, Cartier to Curé Labelle, May 20, 1860, Labelle to H. Langevin, April 3, 1865; Archives du Séminaire de Québec, Cartier to Mgr. Marquis, April 24, 1867; for other examples of clerical lobbying, see William Ryan, *The Clergy and Economic Growth in Quebec, 1896-1914* (Quebec: Les presses de l'université Laval, 1966) and the author's *Promoters and Politicians: The North-Shore Railways in the History of Quebec, 1854-85* (Toronto: University of Toronto Press, 1978), pp. 30-37.

85. *La Minerve*, March 29, April 12, 1859.

86. ANQ, Chapais Collection, Box 32, letters of Edmond Langevin to Hector Langevin, 1865; Box 22, Archbishop Taschereau to Cartier, February 23, 1872.

87. Nadia Eid places ultramontanism in Quebec in the context of the clergy as a social group and their struggle against the "petite bourgeoisie canadienne-française." *Le clergé et le pouvoir politique au Québec* (Montreal: HMH, 1978), p. 11.

88. ASSM, tiroir 99, Correspondance Bishop Bourget and Sulpician Superior, Bourget to C. Doucette, July 3, 1858. Strong pro-ultramontane interpretations are given in Léon Pouliot's study of Bourget (Montreal: Bellarmin, 1972) and in volume two of Rumilly's *Histoire de Montréal* (Montreal: Fides, 1970).

89. ASSM, Correspondance Bishop Bourget and M.D. Granet, Bourget to Granet, October 25, 1863.

90. Ibid., tiroir 100, memorandum 43, May 24, 1867; see also tiroir 99, letter 45, October 19, 1866.

91. Compare, for example, the minutes of the Canadian and London boards, PAC, R.G. 30, vol. 1000, Grand Trunk Minute Book: Canadian Board and vol. 1002, Grand Trunk Minute Book: London Board.

92. Minutes, Canadian Board, May 1856, January 1858; Robert Fulford, *Glyn's: 1753-1953* (London: Macmillan, 1953), pp. 150-55.

93. See PAC, MG 24, Baring Papers, D 21, vol. 150, Baring to Cartier, March 13, May 14, 1862; ANQ, Chapais Collection, C. J. Brydges to Cartier, February 13, 1871. Alan Dever brought to my attention the presence of Cartier correspondence in the Baring papers.

94. PAC, R.G. 30, Canadian National Railway, Edward Watkins to C. J. Brydges, December 12, 1861. The standard histories of the Grand Trunk are A. W. Currie, *The Grand Trunk Railway of Canada* (Toronto: University of Toronto Press, 1957) and G. R. Stevens, *The Canadian National Railways* (Toronto: Clarke Irwin, 1960).

95. Currie, *The Grand Trunk Railway of Canada,* p. 36.

96. In 1854 the Grand Trunk paid both La Fontaine (£37) and Macdonald (£45). PAC, Canadian National Railway, R.G. 30, vol.1973, Grand Trunk ledger, 1853−57.

97. Tom Naylor, *History of Canadian Business, 1867-1914* (Toronto: James Lorimer, 1975), 1:279.

98. Boyd, pp. 161, 25; *La Minerve,* March 12, 1853; *Discours,* p. 49.

99. *Discours,* p. 6.

100. Ibid., p.15.

101. *La Minerve,* July 31, 1866, cited in Louis Richer file, Parks Canada (Quebec City).

102. House of Commons *Debates,* November 25, 1867.

103. *La Minerve,* February 9, 1855.

104. Ibid., October 24, 1852.

105. *Statutes of Canada,* 16 Vic., cap. 37, November 10, 1852.

106. *Le Pays,* September 30, 1852.

107. PAC, R.G. 30, vol. 1000, Minutes of Canadian Board, July 11, 1853; vol. 1002, Minutes, London Board, August 31, 1853; *Journals of Legislative Assembly,* vol. 15, app. 6-7, question 223, quotes $10,000, cited in Louis Richer file, Parks Canada. Board minutes make mention only of legal fees of £340 that were paid to Cartier on May 28, 1856.

108. McCord, acte de société, Cartier et Pominville . . ., March 5, 1859.

109. DCP, M Grant to Cartier, September 24, 1868; J. Hickson to Cartier, May 23, 1872.

110. DCP, Grand Trunk 7 per cent debentures, 1859 (see table 3).

111. Canadian Board Minutes, September 27, 1853; London Board minutes, February 14, 1872.

112. DCP, John Ross memorandum on branch line to Arthabaska, August 20, 1858.

113. R.G. 30, vol. 10186, February 9, 1855.

114. Ibid., vol. 10193, J. Hickson to Cartier, August 21, 1863.

115. Ibid., vol. 1973, ledger, Grand Trunk Railway, 1853−57, May 31, 1861; vol. 10194, minutes, London Board, February 14, 1872.

116. Best, p. 148.

117. DCP, Pominville to Cartier, July 16, 1864; the governor general's niece passed the accident site a few days later: "We had a very pleasant journey to

Montreal. We passed over a drawbridge where a most frightful accident had happened a few days before. The bridge by some carelessness had been left open and a train full of poor German emigrants went down into the river, and a hundred were killed. It gave me a thrill of horror to pass over it." Francis Monck, *My Canadian Leaves* (London: 1891), p.27; Margaret Heap, "La grève des charretiers à Montréal, 1864," *RHAF* 31, no. 3 (December 1977): 371-95.

118. An opposition attempt to deny committee seats to members with railway interests was rejected by the government. *Le Pays*, September 26, 1854.

119. *Statutes of Canada*, 16 Vic., cap. 37, November 10, 1852.

120. Ibid., 18 Vic., cap. 33, December 18, 1854.

121. Currie, *Grand Trunk Railway Company of Canda*, p. 49.

122. Minutes, Canadian Board, June 10, 1859; McCord, Cartier to Alexander Galt, October 1, 1861.

123. Currie, *Grand Trunk Railway Company of Canada*, p. 91; *Discours*, May 2, 1861, p. 285.

124. E. Watkins, *Canada and the States* (London, 1887), p. 497; *Statutes of Canada*, 25 Vic., cap. 56, "Act for the Reorganization of the Grand Trunk Railway," June 9, 1862; PAC, M.G. 24, Baring Papers, D21, vol. 150, Thomas Baring to Cartier, March 13, May 14, 1862.

125. Boyd, p. 22.

126. *La Minerve*, November 29, 1851.

127. R.G. 30, vol. 1973, Grand Trunk ledger, 1853-57.

128. Ibid., vol. 10199, Thomas Blackwell to Thomas Baring, n.d.; for the docks, see ANQ, Chapais Collection, Box 7, C.J. Brydges to Cartier, February 13, 1871; for railways to the north of Montreal, see the role of Cartier's allies, Maurice Cuvillier and Henry Starnes, in the Montreal and St. Jérôme Colonization Railway, a company formed in opposition to the Montreal Colonization Railway, Montreal *Gazette*, February 14, 1872.

129. Joseph-Edouard Turcotte of Three Rivers, quoted in Montreal *Gazette*, May 5, 1855.

130. *Le Courrier du Canada*, April 7, 1857.

131. Montreal *Gazette*, May 12, 1855.

Notes to Conclusion

1. Cartier, Riel, and French-Canadian emigration to the west are discussed in Jane Graham, "The Riel Amnesty and the Liberal Party in Central Canada, 1869-75" (M.A. thesis, Queen's University, 1967) and in Arthur Silver, "French Canada and the Prairie Frontier, 1870-90," *Canadian Historical Review* 50, no. 1 (March 1969): 11-36.

2. Andrée Desilets, *Hector-Louis Langevin: Un père de la Confédération canadienne, 1826-1906* (Quebec: Les presses de l'université Laval, 1969), p.228.

3. *Le Nouveau Monde*, February 6, June 20, 1872.

4. *Mandements, lettres pastorales, circulaires et autres documents* (Montreal, 1887), 6:275, July 25, 1872.

5. *Le Nouveau Monde*, June 1, 1872.

6. *Le National*, May 16, 1872.

7. Boyd, p. 313.

8. W.L. Morton, *The Critical Years: The Union of British North America, 1857-73* (Toronto: McClelland and Stewart, 1964), pp. 247-48.

9. ANQ, Chapais Collection, C.J. Brydges to Cartier, March 5, 1872.

10. *Royal Commission on the Canadian Pacific Railway* (Ottawa, 1873), Alian to G.W. Cass, p. 212. This report is the best source for the effect of the Pacific Railway on the election of 1872. For a full treatment of Allan, see his biography in *DCB*, vol. 11 (forthcoming).

11. Montreal *Gazette*, February 17, 1872.

12. *Le Nouveau Monde*, October 23, 28, November 2, 1871.

13. See B. Young, *Promoters and Politicians: The North-Shore Railways in the History of Quebec, 1854-85* (Toronto: University of Toronto Press, 1978), chap. 3.

14. *Mandements, lettres pastorales et circulaires et autres documents* (Quebec, 1889) 5:116, June 1, 1872; Rumilly, *Histoire de la province de Québec* (Montreal: Fides, 1971), p. 224.

15. *Royal Commission on the Pacific Railway*, Allan to G. E. McMullen, p. 210; testimony of Allan, p. 145. Some of Allan's campaign contributions may have been deposited to Cartier's personal account. Between April and September Cartier deposited $7,268 to his Cuvillier account to pay off amounts owing on stocks. DCP, Sir George Cartier in account with Cuvillier and Company, 1870-73.

16. Rumilly, *Monseigneur Laflèche et son temps* (Montreal: Les Editions Zodiaque, 1938) p. 71.

17. Benjamin Sulte, "Sir George-Etienne Cartier," Gérard Malchelosse, ed., *Mélanges historiques* (Montreal, 1914-28), p.12; ANQ, Chapais Collection, Box 22, Bishop Taché to Cartier, September 14, 1872.

18. Joseph Pope, *Memoirs of the Right Honorable Sir John Alexander Macdonald G.C.B., First Prime Minister of the Dominion of Canada* (London, 1894), 2: 157, J. A. Macdonald to Lord Lisgar, September 2, 1872; Chapais Collection, Box 10, Arthur Dansereau to Hector Langevin, September 7, 1872.

19. PAC, Cartier Papers, P.Winter to Cartier, September 26, 1872; F. C. Bonneau to Cartier, September 10, 1872; V.P. Lavalée to Cartier, September 6, 1872.

20. Ibid., unidentified newspaper clippings, August 28, September 6, 1872.

21. Ibid., Cartier to Louis Archambault, published in *La Minerve*, September 25, 1872.

22. Macdonald to Lord Lisgar, September 2, 1872, quoted in Best, p.584; Chapais Collection, Box 10, A. Dansereau to H. Langevin, September 7, 1872.

23. Alfred Loomis, *Lectures on Diseases of the Respiratory Organs, Heart and Kidneys* (London, 1875).

24. W. H. Dickinson, *On the Pathology and Treatment of Albuminia* (London, 1868).

25. Hortense Cartier diary, December 25, 1872.

26. PAC, Macdonald Papers, no. 85729-31, Josephine Cartier to Macdonald, May 22, 1873; DCP, Cartier to Georgina Ruffenstein, March 13, 1873; Pope, *Memoirs of Sir John A. Macdonald*, 2: 326-27.

27. Macdonald Papers, no.85729-31, Josephine Cartier to Macdonald, May 22, 1873.

28. ASSM, correspondance, John Rose to Macdonald, May 28, 1873.

29. *La Minerve*, June 10, 1873.

30. Lady Dufferin, *My Canadian Journal, 1872-8* (New York, 1891), p. 76.

31. Full details of the funeral were given in *La Minerve*, June 13, 1873, and the Montreal *Gazette*, June 14, 1873.

32. *Le Nouveau Monde*, May 21, 1873, quoted in *La Minerve*, June 16, 1873.

33. This may be compared to what John Foster calls the "packing" of bourgeois communities. *Class Struggle and the Industrial Revolution: Early Industrial Capitalism in Three English Towns* (London: Methuen, 1977), p.182.

34. McCord, St. Jean Baptiste Society receipts, 1846-48.

35. In 1868 Galt asked Cartier if he could arrange a $20,000 loan for him from Clara Symes. DCP, Galt to Cartier, March 1, 1868.

36. For changes in the parish record-keeping system see articles 54-56, 64-65 of the civil code as well as Gérard Bouchard and André Larose, "La réglementation du contenu des actes de baptême, mariage, sépulture, au Québec, des origines à nos jours," *RHAF* 30, no. 1 (June 1976): 67-84; PAC, R.G. 30, vol. 10199, no. 297, *Canada Gazette*, February 23, 1867. For Cartier's support for provincial police, see M. Hamelin, ed., *Debates of the Legislative Assembly of Quebec* (Quebec: *Journal des Débats*, 1974), p. 126.

37. One example of the "mediator" can be seen in Charles Tilly, *The Vendée: A Sociological Analysis of the Counter-Revolution of 1793* (New York: John Wiley and Sons, 1967), p.60; for a discussion of legitimization, see W.L. Guttsman, *The British Political Elite* (New York: Basic Books, 1963), pp. 60-68.

38. Thomas McCord, *The Civil Code of Lower Canada* (Montreal: Dawson Brothers, 1867), p.11; Alexander Galt speech, January 1, 1860, quoted in Isaac Buchanan, *The Relations of the Industry of Canada with the Mother Country and the United States* (Montreal, 1864), p. 315.

39. *Discours*, October 21, 1855, p. 66.

40. Sweeny, p. 176, argues that Cartier was "forced" to borrow money because of "lack of wealth."

Bibliographical Note

Cartier's handwriting was always atrocious and became largely illegible after 1870 as Bright's disease slowly destroyed him. The fate of his papers has intrigued historians. Some of his business records—particularly his fees account book which gives insight into his law practice, 1835 – 53—are in the Château de Ramezay Museum (Montreal) and have been microfilmed by the Public Archives of Canada. A small but important collection of Cartier papers remains in Montreal in the possession of a descendant, Dr. George-Etienne Cartier: these were useful in reconstructing his family and business life. After Cartier's death in London his wife sorted the papers which had been in his possession there into three sections—public affairs, business, and personal. She took the personal papers with her to France, and Cartier's daughter Hortense later donated them to the McCord Museum in Montreal (see McCord Papers, Correspondence file, Hortense Cartier and David Ross McCord, n.d.). Although unorganized, this collection is an important source for Cartier's private life and legal career.

Given Cartier's importance in the Pacific scandal, the Macdonald government showed considerable discretion in disposing of his papers. The public affairs papers left in London were sent by John Rose to John A. Macdonald; they have never been found (see ASSM, Carton 27, Sec. 14, Dossier 9, John Rose to B. Lane, May 28, 1873). In July 1873 two of Cartier's executors—his brother and a notary—visited Ottawa to inventory his belongings. After meeting with Macdonald, they were joined by Hector Langevin who offered his "personal service" out of "friendship and respect for the late Sir George." The three men spent three afternoons and evenings sorting Cartier's papers "which were very numerous." Official and political papers were delivered to Langevin's office; they have never been found. Family papers were sent to Lady Cartier and may form part of the collections in the possession of Dr. George-Etienne Cartier or the McCord Museum. The notary's report explains the fate of the rest: "all papers of a private nature and of no more use were faithfully destroyed" (see

DCP, Inventory of Estate of Cartier, p. 109, Joseph H. Jobin, July 15, 1873).

Because of these major gaps in his private papers much of Cartier's career must be reconstructed from newspapers, legislative debates, government or institutional documents, and the papers of his contemporaries. *La Minerve* faithfully reflected his point of view after the 1840s, while the Montreal *Gazette* after 1853 was generally favourable to Cartier, economic development, and ethnic cooperation. The opposition point of view in Montreal is easily accessible in *Le Pays* and *L'Union Nationale* for the Confederation period, and in *Le National* for Cartier's later career. *Le Nouveau Monde* is useful for Bishop Bourget's position, 1867–73, and *le programme catholique*. Two institutional collections proved valuable. The records of the Seminary of Montreal form a magnificent religious, social, and business collection; the Grand Trunk Railway records are in the Public Archives of Canada.

Cartier's major speeches were collected in *Discours de Sir Georges Cartier*, edited by Joseph Tassé (Montreal, 1893). Several biographies of Cartier exist. John Boyd's *Sir George Etienne Cartier, Bart., His Life and Times: A Political History of Canada from 1814 until 1873* (Toronto: Macmillan, 1914) is a highly favourable description that was published to coincide with the centenary of Cartier's birth. L. O. David's *Biographies et portraits* (Montreal: Beauchemin et Valois, 1876), Alfred Duclos de Celles' *Cartier et son temps* (Montreal: Champlain Collection, 1913), and Benjamin Sulte's "Sir George Cartier," in *Mélanges historiques*, edited by Gérard Malchelosse, 21 vols. (Montreal, 1918–34), are part of this laudatory tradition. H. B. M. Best's "George-Etienne Cartier" (Ph.D. thesis, Laval University, 1969) and Jean-Charles Bonenfant's biography of Cartier in volume ten of the *Dictionary of Canadian Biography* (Toronto: University of Toronto Press, 1972) form the standard recent interpretations of Cartier, emphasizing his pan-Canadianism and federalism. Alastair Sweeny's *George-Etienne Cartier* (Toronto: McClelland and Stewart, 1976) surpasses biographers in his praise for Cartier as "a great national hero," and a great Canadian "playing out his magnificent role." His Cartier has little in common with the Montreal bourgeois depicted in this volume.

In place of a comprehensive bibliography for the period, full references are given in the notes. Extensive bibliographies dealing with Cartier's political milieu are included in W. L. Morton, *The Critical Years: The Union of British North America, 1857-73* (Toronto: McClelland and Stewart, 1971), P. B. Waite, *Canada, 1874-96: Arduous Destiny* (Toronto: McClelland and Stewart, 1971), and Andrée Desilets, *Hector-Louis Langevin: Un père de la Confédération canadienne (1826-1906)* (Quebec: Les presses de l'université Laval, 1969). Bibliographical material on Cartier's Liberal opponents can be found in Jean-Paul Bernard, *Les Rouges: libéralisme, nationalisme et anticléricalisme au milieu du XIXe siècle* (Montreal: Les presses de l'université du Québec, 1971). For sources dealing with Montreal see Paul-André Linteau and Jean Thierge, *Montréal au 19e siècle: bibliographie* (Montreal: Groupe de recherche sur la société montréalaise au 19ᵉ siécle, 1973).

Index

Numbers in italics indicate plates and figures